How To Make A Million Dollars
Part Time and Retire Early

How To Make A Million Dollars Part Time and Retire Early

Damon D Moats

ISBN: 1507856423
ISBN 13: 9781507856420

Table of Contents

Acknowledgments

This book is dedicated to those great people from all over the world who have allowed me to recruit, train, educate, motivate, and work alongside them in network marketing for the past twenty years. I want to thank those family members and friends who never grew tired of me sharing my excitement about my next business venture with them and who supported me in each and every one of those ventures. I really want to thank those distributors who became leaders on our teams, as they often were my source of inspiration. Our dreams and aspirations grew as we got to know one another better, and we actually became family.

It has been said that the two most important days of a person's life are:

The day that you were born and
The day you know why.
— Author unknown

Introduction

This book isn't a sales pitch—it isn't an expensive e-book designed to sell you a useless system that doesn't work. It is a simple, straightforward guide to building a successful network marketing/multilevel marketing (MLM) business. Network marketing isn't a get–rich–quick scheme; however, there are many people who would never have become rich or wealthy without it.

A lot of hard work is involved in building a successful business, regardless of the product, the distribution system, or marketing channel (e.g., storefront, brick–and–mortar, online, or even door–to–door) you choose. If anyone tells you otherwise, run. Schemes and scams are clever and often intentional plans to do or obtain something dishonestly that may injure or harm others. But selling massive quantities of goods and services that the American public wants to buy from you or someone else—and becoming rich and/or wealthy as a result of your hard work—is the American way!

This book contains no secret formulas. There are no shortcuts that can replace the hard work and dedication that you will need to build your business. This book was written to appeal to those people who are interested in knowing how to become financially successful in the network marketing arena, especially those people who have been experimenting with various products and working in different network marketing companies who find that something still is just not clicking.

You believe in the industry and know that it has worked out well for so many people that you know or have heard of. However, you have not yet been able to crack the code, to reach that $5,000–$10,000 per month in income level from your team, part–time, in addition to the income you receive from your full–time job. That is the goal of this book, to get you to that level, that $5,000–$10,000 part–time income level that you are receiving from your team in addition to the income you earn from your full–time job. The point that you want to reach is that moment when you may have 99 problems in life, but money won't be one of them. This book will also be a resource for those people who want to make a major financial shift in their lives in general.

You may have been proactive in reading a lot of books and attending many high–priced financial seminars, just as I did. Those speakers usually want to tell you how to invest your money. For example, they want to tell you whether you should be buying call options or selling put options (a Call option is a security that gives the owner the right to buy one hundred shares of a stock or an index at a certain price by a certain date, and a Put option is a security that you buy when you think the price of a stock or index is going to go down, per the OIC, or options industry council, website). Or they might want to inform you about any number of other garden–variety investments such as purchasing rental real estate or investing in other people's businesses. They may also advise you that you should always pay yourself first and that you must have a rainy–day fund for emergencies.

That's fine, but where is the book that tells people like you and me how to make the money in the first place so that all those how–to–invest–and–budget–my–money books and seminars are even worth reading or attending? Well, I certainly hope that *How to Make a Million Dollars Part Time and Retire Early* will become one of the arrows in your quiver, one that you can use to determine where and how to earn money so that you acquire the wealth that all of those other books want to tell you how to manage once you do have it.

There is nothing in this book that you couldn't figure out through trial and error, but please allow me to save you some time and frustration. This book can be a road map to your success and financial freedom, should you choose network marketing or entrepreneurship in general as one of your paths to wealth and riches. The principles of entrepreneurship apply across the board. This book is designed for beginning network marketers and great upline leaders alike, and will be a tremendous asset to big-business builders seeking a resource to recommend to everyone on their team who wants to get to where they are—the top!

This how-to book will be a very valuable commodity in your team's arsenal—especially for those who want to become professional network marketers. It will show the new network marketer how to choose an upline leader and mentor to work with. It will also teach new or current network marketers how to become so valuable to your upline leaders that your upline leaders will always look out for the welfare and financial success of their new star business partner, you. A major part of why I have written this book is that my teams and I have put over ten thousand distributors into three different network marketing companies with three totally different product lines and three totally new teams in each one. It usually took us less than 24 months each time to build a team of over 10,000 distributors in each of those companies.

As a result, I have encountered tens of thousands of people and I have personally mentored hundreds, if not thousands, of them through the years. Though many are in different network marketing companies today, I still get the "how do I choose a comp plan?" and "how do I build my team?" calls from people every week, as I have for the past ten years or more. I always make time for those calls because I am so passionate about the industry, and because I always like to see people become successful in network marketing so that they can become a shining example for others.

When you become financially successful in network marketing, it will be critical for you to get your story out to combat those cynical friends or pessimistic family members who may have told you emphatically that they were not interested in what you were doing, and in some cases they didn't want to support your efforts even if that just meant sampling your products. They may sing a different tune when they see that you have retired early. They may have laughed at you and stopped taking your calls years ago when you were trying to recruit them into one of the companies that you were working with at the time.

Then comes the day, and I remember it well, when the doubters have caught the vision with some other network marketing company that you are not involved with, of course, and suddenly they are on fire and trying to recruit you onto their team. This happens all the time. Your financial success made them a believer in the network marketing industry, but oddly enough, rather than telling you that you were correct and joining you in your current business, they have joined another company. This is why you, the professional network marketer, will always understand that no doesn't always mean no, but that most often no just simply means "not right now."

Unfortunately, I can usually only give these aspiring network marketers a very limited amount of my time. Hopefully, this book will be the rest of the story or the guidance that these people needed but I didn't have the time to provide. In this book, you will find proof of the successes that my teams and I have enjoyed in the network marketing industry and the strategies we employed to achieve those successes. This secret sauce, if you will, has enabled us to put thousands of people into business in relatively short periods of time. I would love to help you do the same!

CHAPTER 1

Who Am I?

My name is Damon D. Moats, and I have made well over $2 million in commissions in my network marketing career. Most of it I earned working part time, while I was a sales rep with Philip Morris, USA in the early 90's, or a pharmaceutical representative with Mead Johnson Nutrition or Boehringer Ingelheim Pharmaceuticals in the mid–to–late '90s, and on and off during the past fifteen years that I have been a realtor. Shameless plug: I am now the real estate broker/owner of Moats Realty, LLC, and I am licensed in Maryland; Washington, DC; and Virginia (http://www. MoatsRealty.com). I have not yet reached the holy grail of earning $1 million or more in a single year in network marketing, but I do have friends in the industry who have, and I don't plan on slowing down until I do so as well.

I made my first foray into network marketing in 1988, when I purchased a Mary Kay distributorship. When I was a Mary Kay distributor, my goal was to sell cosmetics and other products primarily to the female students on my graduate college campus, which was Bowling Green State University in Bowling Green, Ohio. As a distributor, I hosted a few makeup parties back home in Cincinnati, Ohio, which is where my family lives and where I grew up. However, since I wasn't dedicated to it and didn't take the time to study the industry, I was not very successful with it at that time. I made a few dollars as a distributor, but not enough to quit my day job.

In hindsight, this wasn't really a failure. Today, I actually look at this initial experience as merely a precursor to the success that I would have later in the industry. At the time, I was happy with the fact that I had at least tried. Today, the business schools at Bowling Green or Kentucky State University—where I completed my undergraduate degree—should be teaching something about being a professional network marketer as a part of their business schools curriculums. It can be a very rewarding career path.

In 1990, a year after I graduated from Bowling Green, I was residing in the Washington, DC, metropolitan area. A co-worker there convinced me to give the industry a second go with a multi-level marketing (MLM) company named NSA Water Filters. I was a little more dedicated to this company than I had been to Mary Kay, but I floundered again because I found that I didn't have a strong sponsor, the person who brought me into the business. And I didn't have a strong upline leader, the person who brought my sponsor into the business.

As a matter of fact, I have to apologize to my great friend Mark Holland, a very successful engineer and pastor who came into NSA Water Filters with me. Mark was so serious about being successful with NSA that he invested an additional $5,000 into the water filters right away.   Unfortunately, I quit and left him without the proper sponsoring support because I didn't feel that I could be successful with the product. NSA was one of the many MLM businesses Mark has joined with me because he has always been such a great supporter, business partner, and visionary.

I think Mark may still be sitting on some of those water filters today. Actually, we both learned a lot during that experience, and our knowledge would serve as yet another pillar in the business foundation that we were both engaged in laying. In NSA, I learned the value of having a strong mentor in the business by watching others who were enjoying success in the company. When asked, they usually said their success occurred because of the support and direction they received from their upline leaders.

I realized that I didn't know everything, or anything, for that matter, about how to build a financially successful and rewarding network marketing downline. I also learned that my passion wouldn't fill the experience gap, and if I was ever going to reach the levels of success that others had, I was going to need strong upline leadership and mentorship. I had just discovered one of the keys to success in this business, and I would look for these attributes the next time I decided to join someone's network marketing team.

In 1995, I got more serious about network marketing. I was working as a pharmaceutical representative for Mead Johnson Nutrition, a subsidiary of Bristol Myers–Squibb and I decided that after some early successes, I actually liked and was good at sales. I was looking for a secondary income stream, as I was growing jaded with corporate jobs and the thought of office jobs altogether—some of you know what I mean.

I really liked my job in the beginning, but after a few years, the corporate tactics began to play out with threats of layoffs and cut-backs. Do you know how stressful it is to sleep at night not knowing whether or not tomorrow you will have a job to pay your bills? Now the shine was off the ball. However, let me be clear, I actually had great managers, super managers that I owe my success to while I was in corporate America who trained me well on how to become a true sales professional, hats off to them, and in that I know that I was very fortunate. My managers, thank goodness, were not an issue; it's just that the systems we were all under had a propensity to make life a little more challenging than we wanted it to be.

I decided I wanted to do work that rewarded me more with commissions or bonuses for every unit or product I sold. I looked into franchising, but I quickly realized that franchises were too expensive for me at the time. There can be substantial start–up costs associated with launching a franchise. Though I had some spare capital, it was not nearly enough to seriously consider the kind of franchise I really wanted to get off the ground. I settled on a network marketing opportunity. The start–up costs and overhead were substantially lower, I would be working from home, and the profit margins had the opportunity to be as good, if not even better, than those of owning a franchise, if I took it seriously.

In 1995, a man named Bob Fields introduced me to a network marketing company, Excel Telecommunications. Excel was a telecommunications and long–distance service provider based out of Dallas, Texas. Bob became my good friend. He was a very strong sponsor, and he and I went on to put thousands of people into business with us in Excel. My initial investment was about $500, plus another $500 or so in marketing materials (because I wanted to hit the ground running).

Excel turned out to be more lucrative than I had imagined it would be. My team and I quickly got our incomes up to $3,000 a month (please see the Excel pay stub in exhibit 1) (all exhibits are at the back of the book). Building our businesses part time, which meant in the evenings and on the weekends, was working out well. My early business partners were my neighbors—shout out to the Wood Creek town–home community in Suitland, Maryland, my co–workers, my managers, my fraternity brothers of Omega Psi Phi Fraternity, Inc., friends from college and Aiken High School in Cincinnati and even some of the doctors and nurses that I called on daily as a pharmaceutical sales rep.

In early 1996, my team began to grow very rapidly. My income rose to more than $9,000 a month (please see the Excel pay stub in exhibit 2), and I was still just working the business part time. The telecommunications industry had just been deregulated, and the gold rush for companies entering into this space was on. This industry had heretofore been monopolized by a few industry giants such as AT&T, MCI, and the baby Bell companies. Deregulation of the telecommunications industry simply meant that an average person could start a company and become a reseller and offer discounted pricing to consumers of the exact same long–distance service that we were already paying AT&T and MCI premium dollars for. Except now we had an opportunity to get paid monthly residual commissions when the average customer paid his or her phone bill every month. Our saying was, "Ring Ring = Ching Ching."

Being a reseller of goods and services is how many business owners have amassed their wealth and fortune. Bear in mind that when you go into a nutritional store, drugstore, or grocery store to purchase vitamins, it is highly unlikely that that particular store, which may sell a lot of things, actually manufactures each bottle of vitamins. More often than not, the store selling you vitamins is a reseller of those vitamins, and purchased them from a manufacturer who makes them for everybody. This practice is called white labeling. White labeling occurs when company A (the wholesaler) manufactures a product and then sells it to company B (the retailer), usually with company B's label on it, thus re–branding the product. Company B then sells these products to you and I as if it had actually manufactured them.

Becoming a white–label distributor is as simple as contacting the manufacturer of those vitamins, the name and phone number of which are usually on the back of the bottle in the lower right corner, and buying the product from that company. As long as you can purchase the manufacturer's set quantity minimums, the company will gladly put your business's branded label on the same bottle that it uses for all the other stores up and down the boulevard where you are traveling. In many cases it's exactly the same product, with the same active ingredients, with a different label. The practice of white–labeling is also applied to many services, as well as to consumer products.

In the summer of 1996, I decided to resign from my job and go full time with my Excel business. I figured that I could double my income to $20,000 or even $30,000 per month, as many others had done by going at it full time. Unfortunately, Excel had other plans. A few months later, Excel changed its compensation plan. It changed the number of residential phone service customers that we had to sign up to trigger our bonuses from just two customers to three customers. This seemingly simple change effectively cut everyone's pay in half (please see the Excel pay stub in exhibit 3).

This is why my advice to new distributors is that it may be wiser for you to quit your job and go full time, should you be lucky enough to be faced with that option, after you have $1 million or more in the bank, not before. I started looking for another network marketing company to build wealth with. Excel, which had become a $2 billion corporation within ten years, went public on May 10, 1996; Excel became the youngest company ever to join the New York Stock Exchange (NYSE), trading under the ticker symbol (ECI) (http://en.wikipedia.org/wiki/Excel_Communications). On June 16, 1998, Teleglobe Inc., a global wholesaler of telecommunications services, and Excel Communications Inc., a U.S. long–distance provider, said they had agreed to merge in a $3.2–billion stock swap. The deal combined the global telecommunications services of Montreal–based Teleglobe with the commercial and residential long–distance and paging services that Excel offered in the U.S. Other services the companies provided ranged from telephone calling cards to Internet access (http://articles.latimes.com/1998/jun/16/business/fi–60296).

A former very successful Excel distributor offered me an opportunity to become a co–founding member in a start–up network marketing company that he and some of his other business partners were leaving Excel to launch. This company became known as Maxxis 2000, Inc., and was based in Atlanta, Georgia—it became a very successful network marketing company for about five years or so. I didn't want to go back to the corporate grind, so I accepted. My friend Bernard Porter recruited me into Maxxis 2000 in 1997. Our team went on to become the number one income earners for this company one year later, in 1998. In my best month, I earned over $50,000 (please see the Money Maker's Monthly profile in exhibit 4).

Many other members on our team had $20,000–$30,000 best months as well. These large checks usually came about due to various promotions that Maxxis 2000 ran from time to time. However, all of my leaders continued to work their Maxxis businesses part-time, still working and keeping their day jobs and/or their other businesses. I shared my previous experience with them about leaving my job to go into the business full time way too early and suggested that they stay part-time until they had saved at least $1 million or so before they considered going full time into network marketing.

By the year 2000, Maxxis had grown to over forty thousand distributors, and approximately 25 percent of them were in our organization (please see exhibits 4 and 5). As you can see, my 665–page organizational report—yes, 665 pages—would be printed out from the corporate office in Atlanta and mailed to me each month in a box (a practice now made obsolete by technology). This report shows that we were fortunate enough to have thousands of distributors join our team.

Although Maxxis eventually went out of business, I now had the experience of starting a network marketing company from scratch and our team was an integral part of developing the company distributor base from nothing to over forty thousand reps. Our team alone was generating millions of dollars in monthly sales revenue. My hat goes off to all the hard-working men, women, and college students who took the journey with us (please see exhibits 7 and 8).

Maxxis went out of business after I found and shared documentation proving that the founder/owner was fraudulently selling securities to distributors. As best as I can tell, here is how this scheme played out: after working for this company as a distributor or independent representative as we were called, since we were not employees of the company, for a year or so, I realized that the binary compensation plan, the way the owner had it structured, was faulty, and as a result my team and I weren't making nearly the money that we were entitled to. Therefore, as any good leader would do, I went to the founder/owner, not making a big production out of it and laid out my concerns.

He stalled by asking me to bear with him and promising that he would get these matters remedied expeditiously. However, after another year of what I considered dismal payouts to me and my team, I went back to work as a pharmaceutical sales rep. My income in Maxxis had dropped down to $10,000 or so monthly, and I would still receive that even after going back to work as long as my team sales volume/production was at that level. However, I didn't leave my first job to make that income; I could make that on my job and in addition to that I could make the same amount, or more, part-time doing network marketing with any number of "legitimate" companies, as I had created a system that worked.

I only left my first job to reach my goal of earning $1 million or more annually in network marketing as I had seen others do. A few months after I went back to work with my second pharmaceutical company in the late 90s, the owner of Maxxis called me to ask me if I would consider coming back to be a full-time distributor, he stated that he would pay me what I would have earned from my pharmaceutical company for at least 1 year, as well as my income coming in from my Maxxis team, and that this time he would sincerely endeavor to implement a workable compensation plan that was fair to everyone. I agreed to his terms and left my job.

A year or so after quitting my second job to work Maxxis fulltime, we realized that the owner was not really interested in improving the compensation plan for the field. Simultaneously the company's financials came out on www.hoover.com (you may still be able to find them there today). I decided to read them to see if the representations the owner was telling us in the field and that we were repeating to our prospects were accurate.

For instance, he claimed over and over to us that with the incredible amount of money the company was making that we had purchased our own long distance switch, which would have allowed him to cut expenses in our long distance company and would give him even more money to pay to the distributors. He also claimed over and over that the business was debt free. However, the financial filings showed that Maxxis was actually renting the long distance switch from another business and that those payments to them were in arrears and the company financially would probably not be able to make it through another quarter. Where had the millions of dollars in stock purchases in addition to the millions of dollars in revenues from the sale of the companies products gone?

The financials, as you will see in the public filing at www. hoovers.com, also showed that Maxxis Group was actually owned by him and one other person. This was critical since per his direction to me and all of the distributors around the country who were purchasing company stock that we were to make our checks out to Maxxis Group, not Maxxis 2000. I immediately went to meet with the owner to express my concerns, especially my concern that members of my team and I had been writing checks, per the his direction, to purchase stock in Maxxis 2000 by writing those checks out to Maxxis Group, not Maxxis 2000 which was the company name our monthly checks came to us from. The founder's scheme raised millions of dollars in stock purchases from my and other teams around the country by using my financial success as a distributor with the company as bait. He falsely promised the distributors that because we all helped to build the company that we could now purchase stock in the company before the company went public and that we would all participate in the gains when the stock share price increased significantly from the price we paid for our shares once the company stock was publicly traded.

We must put this into context, the scam happened in the late 90s and early 2000's, before the stock markets crashed when every investor and even non-investor wanted to be a part of an IPO (initial public offering) of any company. Many people on our team and other teams around the country, from me to senior citizens and college students, after being sold on the financial up-side by the owner, individually invested thousands, and many of us invested tens of thousands of dollars in Maxxis stock. The owner was quite shrewd to use my and a few other top distributors financial success with the company compensation plan as the lure to convince all of us to buy what was essentially worthless paper.

I was incensed. At our meeting, after I went through all of my concerns, the owner actually looked me dead in the eye, and said, "If you don't like what I am doing, then start your own company." Stunned, I decided to leave and go to another company, but not before faxing the proof of the con around the country to every distributor who called me to ask me what was going on with Maxxis. When I discovered the scheme, I immediately blew the whistle. Although as any "good" con-artist would do, the owner had a defensive plan that resulted in hardly any of these distributors/investors ever receiving a penny of their hard earned money back. Shortly thereafter the company went out of business. Unfortunately, most of those millions paid to Maxxis Group by fellow distributors all over the country to purchase shares of stock in Maxxis were never to be seen again.

The reality, which I didn't figure out until after I left the company, was quite different. The owner never really intended to actually take the company public. To that end he realized that he could not maintain the illusion he was selling to other distributors around the country that his number one income earner, me, was consistently earning tens of thousands of dollars monthly from the company compensation plan if they knew that I had gone back to a J-O-B as we called it. Therefore, he figured that paying me an additional one or two hundred thousand dollars was a cheap investment that would allow him to continue to sell stock to distributors for another year or two, raising millions more using my story as the bait. He had to act quickly because the word was starting to spread (which was the truth) that I had gone back to work because my team and I weren't making the money that our massive sales production justified.

After I decided to return to Maxxis full-time he also began to advertise the money I was making on our national conference calls without properly splitting it into two parts as per our agreement. I don't have a problem with a network marketing company or any other type of company for that matter deciding to provide additional compensation to top distributors or sales people who can generate a huge team and huge sales quickly to help them to get their company off the ground, it happens everyday and may even keep a company from going under. However, truthful disclosure about those receiving this additional compensation would give distributors a more realistic view of the incomes they could aspire to in that company based on the compensation plan alone.

CHAPTER 2

Wealthy vs. Rich

Most people in America will have the opportunity to become wealthy at some point in his or her lifetime. Some will have a much easier time of achieving this than others, based on a whole host of factors. Regardless of those factors, wealth is still achievable at some point in a good number of U.S citizen's lives, if they learn to surround themselves with the right network of people. I believe that becoming wealthy should not be considered optional for you and your family, but mandatory. Achieving that goal is what building a successful network marketing team is about.

What Is the Difference Between Becoming Rich and Becoming Wealthy?

Simply put, becoming rich means that you have amassed enough money such that making more money, paying your bills, and living the type of lifestyle that you so desire has been taken care of. When you become rich, these are not your daily or even monthly concerns.

However, even if you are rich, you know that you cannot afford a major financial setback. This means that if the setback is significant enough (e.g. an NFL player's career–ending injury in last

Sunday's football game), these concerns could come flooding back, and you could become upper middle class, middle class, or even poor all over again.

Take, for example, the majority of retired pro football players. It is said that the average pro football player's career averages four to six years. As a result, many of these individuals—who have created high-flying lifestyles while active in the league—may have significant financial problems after being forced to retire too early. Many of them often have to get regular nine-to-five jobs within a few years of leaving the NFL because they were rich, not wealthy. Remember, I said that they had to get nine-to-five jobs after leaving the NFL, not that they wanted to return to the workforce.

Getting a nine-to-five job because you want to, not because you have to, is certainly an acceptable choice after you have enjoyed a high level of financial success. It is much less pleasant if you are forced to do so. Conversely, you may have heard many different stories about NFL team franchise owners, but one story you have yet to hear is the one about the NFL owner who got into so much financial trouble that he or she had to sell his or her team (which has happened) and then go back into the workforce. This is because NFL owners become wealthy rather than just rich.

More than likely, prior to purchasing the team, and due to the ridiculously high valuations placed on the franchises today, the NFL franchise owners already owned some, if not many, income-producing assets, and they were already very wealthy. If you own income- producing assets (restaurants, rental real estate, IT companies, public storage warehouses, etc.) that made you wealthy, then it will take a much greater financial disaster to derail your comfortable lifestyle. Also, if you are actually already wealthy (e.g., Warren Buffet, Bill Gates, Oprah Winfrey, or Tyler Perry), there's practically nothing you could do that would cause you to become working class ever again.

A very successful person once stated that if you remember and execute this simple formula, you can become wealthy in America: "people become wealthy by selling goods and services to the American public, in volume." That last part is the key, volume. Many people think that if they just open the doors or start the company, the people will come. Not so fast, kemosabe. You have to make sure that lots of people want to buy what you are selling. But this is the easy part. Don't make this too difficult. The bottom line is that if you see other people selling something to the American public in volume, chances are you can sell the exact same thing and become wealthy, too.

Look, don't make becoming wealthy so difficult. As a matter of fact, a very wealthy friend once said to me, "Becoming wealthy is sometimes so simple that it's often beneath our comprehension." He was basically saying that people can overanalyze what it takes to become wealthy. He should know—he became wealthy by starting, building, and then selling his trash company to a larger trash company for millions. As he says, "Everyone will make trash that needs to be picked up by someone, forever."

Robert Kiyosaki of *Rich Dad, Poor Dad* fame made the four quadrants of wealth creation fun to learn in his book *The Cashflow Quadrant* and in his game called *CASHFLOW*. I highly recommend that you play his *CASHFLOW* game with your children, starting when they are in about the sixth grade. Then play it regularly for the rest of your life.

Kiyosakis' four quadrants of wealth creation are:

1. Employee — Has a job
2. Self–Employed — Owns a job
3. Business Owner — Owns a system
4. Investor — Owns investments

Another way to articulate the same concept of Kiyosakis' *four quadrants of wealth creation* are the four wealth creation principles that I have been trained on all of my network marketing career, this is how I have explained wealth creation through the years in mentoring my team members and prospects:

The Four Wealth Creation Principles

1. Business ownership: owning a business allows you to create and take additional tax deductions.
2. Asset leveraging: asset leveraging allows you to profit from the efforts of others. J. Paul Getty once famously said, "I would rather earn one percent of 100 people's efforts than 100 percent of my own effort."
3. Residual and royalty income: doing something once and getting paid over and over again. Think of your mobile phone service or utility bills.
4. Red hot trends: marketing those things that are in demand, red hot demand, today!

The transferability of the sales, marketing, and product knowledge training we received in the pharmaceutical sales business is directly attributable to the rapid growth of our teams in each company. Our teams constantly trained to do a two–minute, 15–minute, and 30–minute presentation. You always want to be respectful of a prospect's time because that is where your wealth in this business will come from.

Quiz: Who is wealthy and who is rich in the following examples, and who would you rather be?

Example 1: John works for a software company in New Haven, Connecticut, and is a software engineer who makes approximately $450,000 annually. John has a pretty luxurious lifestyle—a new home with a mortgage, a boat, a lake house, etc. Once John has met all of his financial obligations, he has about $20,000 left over at the end of the year.

On the other hand, Dionna is a real estate investor with twenty paid-off rental properties in Cincinnati, Ohio, in low-to-moderate-income neighborhoods. She averages about $800 profit per month from each property, about $16,000 a month, and $192,000 per year. Dionna makes about $62,000 per year working as an auditor for the city of Cincinnati. She has been buying modestly priced rental properties for the past ten years. Dionna's personal home is paid for, and at the end of each year, after Dionna has met all her financial obligations, she has about $150,000 left over.

Example 2: Rob is a high-powered attorney working for a law firm in Washington, D.C. Rob makes about $525,000 per year from his job, and he lives the D.C. lifestyle of the rich and famous. After Rob has met all his financial obligations each year, he has about $30,000 left over.

On the other hand, Steve has forty gumball machines in Richmond, Virginia, in restaurants, barbershops, and churches, which average about $500 per month after expenses—in total, Steve makes approximately $20,000 monthly from his gumball machines and $240,000 annually. He's been buying gumball machines for twenty years now. Steve makes about $75,000 per year at his job as an exterminator. Steve's home has a small mortgage of about $60,000 with a $455 monthly payment, and his cars are paid for. After Steve has paid all his financial obligations at the end of the year, he has about $200,000 left over.

Example 3: Karen is corporate vice president for GE in Chicago. She makes $435,000 per year, lives downtown on the waterfront, travels well, and has about $25,000 left over at the end of the year after she has met all her financial obligations.

On the other hand, Taylor is a pediatrician for Kaiser in Houston, Texas, and makes about $120,000 per year. However, Taylor has been operating a part-time multilevel vitamin business for the past ten years. She has built a solid team. Her part-time business brings in $25,000 per month and $300,000 annually. Taylor doesn't have a car note because she has qualified for the last seven years for the multilevel marketing company's car program, which pays for a brand new car every three years. Taylor's house has a modest mortgage of $90,000 with a $600 per month payment. At the end of the year after Taylor has paid all her financial obligations, she has about $225,000 left over.

Wealth simply means that you have built an income–producing asset that pays for your lifestyle whether you decide to go to work or not. Having the choice or the option is what is of utmost importance. Wouldn't you agree?

CHAPTER 3

Show Me the Money

The corporate and financial summary information for each of the companies discussed in this chapter can be found at Forbes.com, Businessforhome.org, Prnewswire.com, Direct Selling News.com, or on the individual companies' websites.

Hopefully, you will be even more open to investigating and trying your hand at some of the great opportunities to earn additional income or even become wealthy in the network marketing industry once you have digested the revenues of the companies that are highlighted in this chapter. Remember, these companies were built by people just like you and me. No, not everyone who joins and builds a business in a network marketing company is going to get rich, but being rich can be a relative thing.

For example, you might talk to a father who was having a tough time providing for his family every month until he joined a network marketing company. Now, after just two years of part–time organization building, he consistently makes an extra $3,200 each month that pays his family's mortgage, and that could be what it means to be rich to him. Or you might talk to newlyweds who had only been married for a short time after meeting in college but were already drowning in student loan debt repayments until they joined and built, on a part–time basis, a network marketing team. Now, after just one year, they find themselves bringing in an extra $1,700 per month. They now feel comfortable having children, and that could be what it means to be rich to them.

The average person in network marketing may only make an extra couple hundred bucks per month, but that may be all the effort that they are actually willing to put into building the business. But then there are those other people who say they are going to give it all they have for a period of time, say five to ten years, and are able amass a monthly income that rivals that of a pro athlete, but without the concussions. You can choose your destiny.

If one company goes out of business, then you can join another company with your existing team and get back to profitability very quickly. If you got fired from your job, you wouldn't say, "I'm never going to work a job again." Nor should you say, "That network marketing company did me wrong; therefore, I'm never doing network marketing again." There's too much money waiting for you, your family, and your friends in the network marketing industry. You are uniquely qualified to win financially, so let's get after it.

Many network marketing companies are making more money than ever before. Many of these companies' enrollments are up significantly. Some people in the industry have attributed the increases to the recession that started in 2006. During the recession, many people lost their jobs; you may even have had some personal experience with this yourself. So, some people who could not find other employment decided to try network marketing as a way to hopefully survive. But because they were so committed and they were lucky enough to pick the right company for themselves, many of their incomes and lifestyles are actually thriving.

Think about it—not many companies today advertise that you should come to work with them and stay for the next thirty years and retire, not even the military. In fact, according to Jeanne Meister, contributing editor for *Forbes*, younger employees stick with one job for only a few years:

"The average worker today stays at each of his or her jobs for 4.4 years, according to the most recent available data from the Bureau of Labor Statistics, but the expected tenure of the workforce's youngest employees is about half that. Ninety–one percent of Millennials (born between 1977–1997) expect to stay in a job for less than three years, according to the Future Workplace "Multiple Generations @ Work" survey of 1,189 employees and 150 managers. That means they would have 15–20 jobs over the course of their working lives!"[1]

This means it may be wise to be flexible going forward with your career choices.

A Sample of Successful Network Marketing Companies

Let's look at just a few of the many companies that have grown so large that they now have many distributors who are earning a few hundred dollars per month from the organizations they have built, and which may have some people earning a few hundred thousand dollars per month.

- **Amway:** the grandparent of modern multilevel marketing. In 2013, Amway set new record sales of $11.8 billion. Industry: household and personal products. Founded: 1959. Country: United States. CEO: Doug DeVos and Steve Van Andel. CFO: Michael Cazer. Website: http://www.amway.com. Employees: 21,000. Headquarters: Ada, Michigan.[2]

---

1 Jeanne Meister, "Job Hopping Is the 'New Normal' for Millennials: Three Ways to Pre–vent a Human Resource Nightmare," *Forbes*, August 14, 2012, http://www.forbes.com/sites/jeannemeister/2012/08/14/job–hopping–is–the–new–normal–for–millennials–three–ways–to–prevent–a–human–resource–nightmare/.

2 http://www.forbes.com/companies/amway/. February 28, 2015.

- **Mary Kay:** Industry: household and personal products. Founded: 1963. Country: United States. CEO: David Holl. CFO: Terry Smith. Website: http://www.marykay.com. Employees: 5,000. Sales ending fiscal year December 31, 2012: $3 billion. Headquarters: Addison, Texas.[3]
- **Avon:** Industry: household and personal care. Founded: 1886. Country: United States. CEO: Sheri McCoy. Website: http://www.avon.com. Employees: 36,700. 2013 sales: $9.98 billion. Headquarters: New York, New York.[4]
- **Nu Skin:** the company's scientific leadership in both skin care and nutrition has established Nu Skin as a premier anti-aging company. 2013 revenue: $3.177 billion, a 49 percent year-over- year improvement. Website: https://www.nuskin.com/en_DE/home.html. In the United States, the Company had an average of 67,740 Active Distributors during 2013. Founded: 1984. CEO: Truman Hunt. Founder: Blake Roney. Headquarters: Provo, Utah.[5]
- **Herbalife:** Industry: food retail. Founded: 1980. Country: Cayman Islands. CEO: Michael Johnson. Website: http://http://www.herbalife.com. Employees: 7,000. 2013 sales: $4.83 billion. Headquarters: George Town, Cayman Islands.[6]
- **Blyth:** Blyth, Inc., is a Greenwich-based marketing and manufacturing company that sells personal and decorative products. The company reported having 4,000 employees as of January 2007 and is incorporated in Delaware. In 2001, it was the largest candle maker in the United States. Subsidiaries include the PartyLite direct sales business and ViSalus, a multi- level marketing company. Net sales for

---

3 http://www.forbes.com/companies/mary-kay/. February 28, 2015.

4 http://www.forbes.com/companies/avon-products/. February 28, 2015.

5 http://www.nuskin.com/corpcom/en_US/newsroom/press_releases1/2014/nu-skin-enterprises-reports-record-2013-annual-and-fourth-quarte.html. February 28, 2015.

6 http://www.forbes.com/companies/herbalife/.com. February 28, 2015.

the three months ended June 30, 2014 were $157.8 million. Founded: 1976. CEO: Robert B. Goergen. Website: http://www.blyth.com. Headquarters: Greenwich, Connecticut.[7]

- **PartyLite:** a company that sells candles, incense, diffusers, sachets, bath products, and decorative accessories for the home. It markets its products through about 17,000 independent consultants in the United States and another 35,000 throughout a dozen markets worldwide, including Australia, Canada, Germany, Mexico, and the United Kingdom. Consultants sell PartyLite's products through home parties held by hostesses and via personalized e-commerce sites. PartyLite also markets breads, cheeses, desserts, sauces, and other snack foods under PartyLite's Two Sisters Gourmet brand. Established in 1973, PartyLite has been owned by Blyth since 1990. 2012 sales: approximately $280 million. Website: http://www.partylite.com.[8]
- **ViSalus:** a multilevel marketing company based in Los Angeles, California, with offices in Troy, Michigan. CEO, Ryan Blair. Co- founders Ryan Blair, Blake Mallen, and Nick Sarnicola. 2012 revenues: $624 million. Website: http://www.visalus.com. The company markets weight–management nutritional products, dietary supplements, and energy drinks in the United States, Canada, and the United Kingdom through a network of approximately 76,000 independent distributors. Weight management products include Vi–Shape meal replacement shake and Vi–Trim Clear Control Drink Mix. ViSalus is also in a partnership with Blyth.[9]

---

7 "Blyth, Inc., Reports 2nd Quarter 2014 Sales and Earnings," PRNewswire, Aug. 1, 2014, http://www.prnewswire.com/news–releases/blyth–inc–reports–2nd–quarter–2014–sales–and–earnings–269526041.html.

8 Ibid.

9 Ibid.

- **It Works Global:** a direct marketer of health supplements, skin care products, and body–shaping aids. The company, founded in Michigan in 2001, moved to Bradenton, Florida, in 2011. It Works currently employs 86 people full time. Founder and CEO: Mark B. Pentecost. Website: http://www.myitworks.com. The new headquarters, which is designed to accommodate up to 150 employees, is the center of a business that sells its products through 90,000 independent distributors in eighteen countries. The company sold $27 million in products in 2010. Sales grew to $456 million in 2013, according to the company.[10]

- **Melaleuca:** a consumer–direct marketing company. Melaleuca announced annual revenues of $1.13 billion for 2012. CEO: Frank VanderSloot. Website: http://www.melaleuca.com. Melaleuca has grown in 26 of the past 27 years, and there continues to be strong consumer demand for Melaleuca's health and wellness products. Melaleuca touts its high–quality natural ingredients, which make up over 350 proprietary and patented formulas. In 1985, Melaleuca launched with what they labeled as a new business model called "consumer–direct marketing," which some say operates just like multilevel marketing but others say that it operates substantially different than multilevel marketing. In Melaleuca's consumer– direct marketing model, there are no distributors who purchase and resell products, and there are no multiple levels of distribution. Instead, marketing executives refer customers directly to the company. Customers then purchase the product directly from the company instead of getting it from a distributor. This means that no one makes any investment in inventory, and there is no way for

---

10   Ted Nuyten, "It Works! Global opens $10 Million HQ: Sales Revenue Up to $456 Million, http://www.businessforhome.org/2014/07/it–works–global–opens–10–million–hq–sales–revenue–up–to–456–million/. February 28, 2015.

anyone to lose money, making operating a Melaleuca business essentially a risk–free venture. Prior to 1985, this concept had never been tried.[11] However, I will say, since I have
a bag of Melaleucas' protein shake in my cabinet which I received when I signed up with my good friend Larry Ballew
out of Cincinnati, which I like, from my experience with the
company, it operates just like every other network marketing company I have ever been a part of.

- **5LINX:** a multilevel marketing company, 5LINX distributes
  long– distance phone services, cellular phones, and accessories through a network of more than 83,000 independent
  sales representatives. The company's product portfolio in-
  cludes several brand names, including wireless products from
  Verizon, T–Mobile, and Sprint Nextel, and now it also markets
  a line of healthcare products and nutrition products. In 2012,
  5LINX had revenue of $104 million, up from $83 million in
  2011. Website: http://www.5linx.com. Cofounder, President,
  and CEO Craig Jerabeck runs 5LINX with cofounders Jeb
  Tyler, executive vice president of marketing, and Jason Guck,
  executive vice president of sales. The company was founded
  in 2001 and has 275 employees.[12] I signed up in 5LINX with
  my long-time networking buddy, Roscoe Campbell.
- **Prepaid Legal Services:** Prepaid Legal was a MLM company founded in 1983 by Harland Stonecipher (no, that's
  not a made–up name). As the story goes, way back in 1969,
  Stonecipher was in a car accident. Frustrated at the lack of
  legal insurance options available at the time, Stonecipher
  started up the Sportsman's Motor Club in 1972 offering
  members "legal expense reimbursement services." The

---

11   Tom J. Kennedy, 2013: A Record–Breaking Year For Melaleuca, Wednesday, February
19, 2014, http://sdi–usuryfree.blogspot.com/2014/02/2013–record–breaking–year–for–
melaleuca.html.

12   "Some Companies Seem to Have It All: Fast–Growing 5LINX® Is One of Them," July 1,
2012, http://directsellingnews.com/index.php/view/fueling_growth_at_5linx#.VRbKbvzF94I.

Sportsman's Motor Club relied on a traditional sales model for eleven years before adopting an MLM–style business model and compensation plan in 1983. Prepaid Legal was born. In 1984, Prepaid Legal went public on the NASDAQ National Market System, and in 1999, it was listed on the New York Stock Exchange, where it remained until 2011. In January 2011, Prepaid Legal and MidOcean Partners agreed to sell Prepaid Legal to MidOcean Partners, a private equity firm. Finally, in September 2011, MidOcean Partners announced that they would be re–branding Prepaid Legal as Legal Shield, the incarnation of the company that still exists today. Website: www.legalshield.com. 2010 revenue: $458.5 million.[13] I signed up in Prepaid Legal with my aunt Pamela Moats-Winston out of Cincinnati.

These are just a handful of the hundreds of companies that have become quite profitable in the network marketing industry. So when your co–worker invites you out to that next opportunity meeting, and I'm sure many of you have been invited to enough network marketing meetings that you know the pitch when you hear it, give your curiosity the permission to say yes. Yes, I will come and at least listen to what has gotten you so excited, because at the very least I want to encourage you to be successful, whether I join the business with you or not. That's support.

---

13 "Pre–Paid Legal Announces 2010 4th Quarter & Year–End Results," PRNewswire, January 4, 2011, http://www.prnewswire.com/news–releases/pre–paid–legal–announces–2010–4th–quarter––year–end– results–112861914.html.

CHAPTER 4

The Keys to Success

n this chapter, we will be discussing the keys to success. These are the principles that you should follow when building your team. These are also the principles you will want to instill in the recruits who become your serious business builders. These principles are simple and straightforward, and if you follow them, you can be very successful in the network marketing industry.

Know Your Why

To be successful in network marketing you must be driven and goal focused. It is imperative that you understand why you are getting involved in this industry and with the company that you have chosen to join. A very clear understanding of your goals and objectives are critical keys to success in every business endeavor. In network marketing, you will face a lot of rejection. Many people will close many doors in your face, and they might even be (and probably will be) friends and family members. This can be very frustrating and disconcerting. It can dishearten and diminish your drive. However, if you are trained to keep your end goal in mind (i.e., how much money you want to make from the business and the lifestyle that you want to live), then this inevitable rejection will be much easier to deal with. People will say no, and that's okay.

People who reject your business are not rejecting you as a person, unless you haven't taken your business seriously and they can see that. Most often people reject the unknown. You probably regularly reject many things that are presented to you, especially if you are unfamiliar with them. Just imagine, you may be presenting your listeners with information and introducing them to people who are making the same amount in a month that other people make in a year.

This certainly could spook a person who doesn't have anyone in his or her network who has been financially successful in the network marketing industry, and such apprehension should be understandable. You may want to spend a little more time getting to know your prospect. Consider how this person may feel if he or she has never been financially successful in any traditional business endeavor that he or she may have embarked upon.

Often an individual's immediate reply is based upon his or her expectation of success or failure in the business. But those expectations may not be shared with you unless you are great at asking probing questions, such as: Have you ever tried to become an entrepreneur? Do you believe that you have what it takes to build a business where you can make the same amount monthly that some people earn annually? Too many people are trained to believe that someone else should have that kind of financial success. They've been convinced, or they convinced themselves, that someone else should be able to retire early, but not them.

To many people, the corporate world, with its good points and bad points, feels safe. They may perceive network marketing or entrepreneurship, with its good points and bad points, as risky. Typically this is only the case if they don't know or have a personal relationship with someone who has become financially liberated via network marketing or other forms of entrepreneurship. If an individual is afraid of success or hard work, then he or she is not a person that you will want to work with when endeavoring to build your team and your business.

Everyone has a Why: something that motivates them to do the things they do. Everyone has a reason to get up in the morning and go to work. Most people are directed by a desire deeper than simply getting by. For me, it was paying off my student loans. It was helping my parents buy a house. My parents are honest, hardworking, traditional people.

For over forty years, they had built their careers, my father as a janitor with UPS and my mother as a homemaker. They had little more than a rental apartment lease to show for it (and six great kids). As their son, if I knew of a better way to build wealth, it was my duty to help make sure that they understood and participated in that better life.

So on those days when more people told me no rather than yes, I learned to concentrate on my Whys. Why was I doing this business in the first place? That kept me motivated and moving forward. When I got frustrated or tired, I thought of my family, and I thought of a better life for myself and for my future family. When I thought of my family, I often found the strength to carry out the things that I needed to do that day to secure financial success in building my team and building my business.

What Is Your Why?

Getting into network marketing is more about the Why than it is about the How. Don't focus on the How. The How will come in time.

The Why will give you the drive to find the How. Here are a few examples:

- Do you want to send your kids to private school, debt free?
- Do you want to send your kids to college, loan free?

- Are your job hours being cut?
- Are you getting laid off from your job?
- Are you unhappy with your career?

Please get a piece of paper and write down your Whys, or write them below.

Write them all down.

1.
2.
3.
4.
5.
6.

Frame your Why list. Make copies and hang them on your walls and mirrors.

Every time that you get scared or uncertain (and you will) and every time that you have a shadow of a doubt (and you will) look at your list of Whys. Look at your Whys as motivational pillars. Draw strength from them. Pour some gasoline on your fire (which is your determination) and become so passionate that people will want to come to watch you burn. Being successful in business is more about emotion and drive than it is about intellect—you can hire intellect. It's much more difficult to hire someone who will stay motivated as long as it takes to become wealthy, whether it takes five years, ten years, twenty years, or a lifetime.

A stalwart will and a passion that burns like a furnace are all you need to make it in network marketing and most businesses, for that matter. Again, you can hire intellect. Now, many of you will bring some exceptional qualitative and quantitative skills to the business—this just simply means that you might become wealthy faster than the average entrepreneur, which is great as well.

Even if you feel that you lack certain skills or knowledge when you begin building your business, be patient and trust the process—these skills or perceived additional levels of knowledge needed to become successful will come from you and your growth and development or from one of your team members over time while you build your network marketing business. If you have the will to force your own change and the drive to push it forward, you will be fine. Complacency is the enemy. Don't become complacent.

When confronted with difficult choices, such as the opportunity to work harder and make more money after you have become somewhat successful in your network marketing business, a part of you may say something like: "We are making enough money; we don't need to put in three more days of work. Let's just put it on cruise control and chill." That may not be the winner in you talking; that may be your fear of excellence talking—that negative mental self–talk that tends to dominate the way we view most of the opportunities we are presented with that must be dealt with swiftly and on a daily basis. You should recognize that you could be on the road to derailing your massive success by taking a break too early.

That small fearful voice inside may unconsciously change your trajectory because that inner voice of complacency may feel safer just being mediocre. Yes, fear is normal, but allowing fear to prevent you from taking action, when taking action is what is required, can certainly sabotage your objectives. Fear can protect us from harm in some cases, but many people train themselves to be fearful and skeptical about most of the decisions they make in life, and what amazes me even more is that some people even brag about it. How many times have you heard someone say, "I'm skeptical of everything," as if it was a badge of courage?

I highly recommend that you read the book Feel the Fear and Do It Anyway, by Susan Jeffers, Ph.D. Dr. Jeffers explains how fear comes over all of us, but the people who ultimately become successful are the people who feel that fear, embrace that fear, and then take action even though they remain fearful. When you have mastered this skill you will find that many things that once made you fearful now look like grand opportunities for your continued success.

Remember, fear and complacency are predators to success. But if you push past that complacency and stay vigilant, you will find the true level of financial success that you and your organization have been seeking. Always remember: about 80 percent of your self–talk is negative. You should try to live by the African proverb that says, "When there is no enemy within, then the enemy without can do you no harm." Stop talking yourself out of greatness. You deserve to do great things.

Take Your Why and Turn It into a Goal

Your goal doesn't have to be huge. Start small and then grow into a bigger goal. At first I wanted to make enough in network marketing each month to cover my student loan payments. When I reached that goal, I expanded my vision. My goal became paying twice the amount of my student loan payment every month.

Then I started making enough to put extra payments down on my home mortgage, and I was able to whittle it down to the point that paying off my mortgage was only a year away. I was only thirty. By setting small, quantifiable goals, I was able to measure my successes and in turn increase my level of belief in myself, which is very important. I could see a change in my financial life. I felt encouraged by the success I was experiencing. I could push forward and seek out larger goals. I motivated myself with small, tangible successes.

Initially, when I started, I determined my Why, and the daily presence of that Why was part of what allowed me to succeed. My Why was paying off my student loans ($30,000), and I was able to do so within nine months of starting my part–time network marketing business. I hated the idea that due to the mounting interest that was accumulating every month; the balance of the student loan would continue to increase rapidly. To me, those student loans hung over my head like a guillotine.

So I decided to make this my goal, paying off my student loans twenty–five years early. To someone who had not been out of college that long, a $30,000 debt was very intimidating. That monthly payment, in addition to my mortgage payment, car payment, and other monthly obligations, was beginning to add unnecessary stress to my life, and I had to find a way to eliminate that stress. Initially, when I looked at the additional payments that I would have to make each month to meet the goal of paying off my student loans, I was a little unsure of myself. Rightfully so! That was a lot of money to me at that time—$30,000 was more than some people were making at their jobs in one year even with a college degree.

But I stayed focused. I knew the other voice in my head, complacency, was the voice telling me to be normal, act like everyone else, and just pay the loan off over the natural life cycle of the loan, thirty years. I believe I actually got scared at one point when I realized that I might be able to reach my goal—that I could actually pay off those student loans within twelve months.

Fear can control any of us, just when we think we are in control. But if you develop and sharpen that positive, motivating voice in your head, you will stay in complete control of your internal messaging and achieve your goals. So I challenged and changed that negative voice in my head to the voice that spoke more positive, motivating words. Then I took it a step further. I set two more Whys. I wanted to help my parents buy a home. I wanted to become financially independent.

Once you realize that you have the power to change your financial status within yourself, you will become very bold. You will decide that you will no longer be beholden to anyone other than yourself for your income. I went on to be able to assist my parents in the purchase of their first home. Don't you think it would be quite liberating to help your parents buy a home, especially if they never had the luxury of owning their own home? Feel free to borrow this Why.

With these Whys in mind and the passion that they will fill you with—the love for your family, the frustration you've had with some of your employers, your desire to no longer be nervous about where your next paycheck is coming from—your mission has begun.

How do you build a business if you've never done that before? Listen—again, don't worry about the How. The How of achieving your goals will take care of itself if you have your Whys clearly etched into your mind. If you can stay motivated, focused, passionate, and dedicated to your cause, then you will have no trouble locating the individuals and the necessary assets to aid you in uncovering the How.

You will learn the How as you go along this journey. All you need is the ability to ask the right questions of the right people who have the applicable information to help you grow your business. This just takes tenacity. There is no shame in not knowing; however, there is shame in not growing. Push yourself to make some new mistakes instead of repeating the same old mistakes time after time.

As you well know, starting a business requires a high level of commitment, desire, and willingness to do as much research as is necessary for you to win financially in network marketing. All of which you can learn by observing and engaging people you admire who are already successful entrepreneurs. It can also be a good thing, sometimes, to start out as a blank slate. That way you can act as a sponge and soak up all the information available on how you are going to win at becoming a successful entrepreneur.

Be Personable

Network marketing will require that you talk to a lot of people, strangers included. Get comfortable with it. Learn to talk to people you don't know. You can go to bookstores, churches, restaurants, bars, and coffee shops, strike up conversations with strangers, try holding their attention and creating a conversation they enjoy, and aim to make a friend first. Keep this old adage in mind: "People don't want to know how much you know until they know how much you care." We all have charisma within ourselves, and sometimes we forget how to access it. Practicing being polite and engaging can translate into making a lot of money in the network marketing industry.

Practice listening. Everybody likes a good listener. Make people feel important. Remember their names and use them. I recommend that you read Dale Carnegie's How to Win Friends and Influence People. Despite being written in the 1930s, it is still full of immensely valuable information about how to interact with people in both a personal and business environment. I would like to draw your attention to a couple of sections in Carnegie's book, in case you are eager to start reading it.

In his book, Carnegie lists six core tenets of being likable:

1. Become genuinely interested in other people.
2. Smile.
3. Remember that a person's name is, to that person, the sweetest and most important sound in any language.
4. Be a good listener and encourage others to talk about themselves first.
5. Talk in terms of the other person's interests.
6. Make the other person feel important, and do it sincerely.

These are not manipulations and they are not methods of tricking someone into liking you. When manipulations work, they do so only for a short period and always leave a bad taste in the manipulated person's mouth. Carnegie's techniques are founded in observations of human behavior, and during my life I have found them to be very astute analyses. The goals of the previously mentioned tenets are to make individuals more receptive to you and your message.

Be Gregarious and Tenacious

Go out and meet people. Talk to people everywhere you go. Even when you are in a bad mood, try to engage others. One of my mentors taught me that we all can break ourselves out of a bad headspace or a negative mind–set by talking to people when we are in a bad mood and at least trying to be pleasant and gregarious. You will quickly learn how to shift yourself into that pleasant place. This will be an invaluable skill throughout your network marketing or entrepreneurial career.

There will be times when you will hit every red light and when everything in your day appears to be going wrong. There will be days when you are feeling frustrated and down, but you will still have to do a presentation and a presenter who is clearly angry at the world around him or her will not be able to positively influence his or her audience. Remembering what is discussed in this book will hopefully help pull you out of that bad mood on those days, and yes, there will be some of those days.

Be tenacious. People will say no, and you will have to move past that. There will be those people who you will want to try to educate about financial literacy, which is what this book really is all about, but I'll have to save some of that for the next book. Sometimes it will be better to just move on to the next person. If you are not tenacious, the rejection will make you give up and go home. And we all know that you cannot become financially successful sitting at home watching cable television.

Understanding the Compensation Plan

You probably wouldn't accept a job before you knew how much you would be paid and when. Then why should you join a network marketing organization without knowing what you have to do in order to get paid? If you earn a higher commission from selling cabbage, then you want to make sure that you are selling as much cabbage as humanly possible. But if your cabbage commission is lower than your carrot commission, then focus on the carrots.

This is pretty straightforward stuff, but most people getting started in network marketing haven't ever seen a compensation plan like a network marketing compensation plan before. Network marketing compensation plans aren't that hard to understand, but they do require a bit of explaining and research to become familiar with the new vocabulary. Network marketing companies use a variety of compensation plans, and they all appeal to different individuals for different reasons.

When you are researching that company that your co–worker invited you out to hear about, you should pick a compensation plan that rewards you for doing something that you are particularly good at or for marketing a product that you can really develop a passion for. If you think of yourself as a strong recruiter, find a plan that focuses on that. If you think that you will be better at direct selling and setting up customers on monthly product auto–ships (a company's program that automatically drafts customers' accounts and then ships them their chosen products on the same date each month), then focus on a plan that offers higher commission rates for those aspects.

I will take you through a more detailed analysis of the various compensation plan structures later in chapter 6. Think about your strengths and weaknesses and prepare yourself for a moment of internal honesty that will help you decide which compensation plans and company product mixes will work best for you and your personality. Most importantly, I hope that you will at least give a couple of the companies in the industry a try. And if the first company that you join and work with later turns out to be a dud for you, then jump on the next one right away—don't delay.

Solicit People with Money

Now, this topic is always a fun subject and an issue that can be very humorous in hindsight, but it is also probably the most important area of focus to understand. When it comes to network marketing, that adage is still true; it takes money to make money.

You see, its okay for you to drive thirty minutes across town to show your prospect your company business opportunity presentation (BOP), and after the prospect has had a chance to digest the information, it's okay for him or her to not be interested in joining the business. But it's not okay if you drive thirty minutes across town to show your prospect your BOP, and after viewing it, the prospect says that she is extremely excited about the opportunity and eagerly wants to join the business with you, but there is one slight problem—it may take three to six months for her to save up the $300 that she needs to join the business with you.

Wait a minute: you didn't tell your prospect the distributor sign–up fee was $30,000, or even $3,000; you said $300. And her response to that was that she was living paycheck to paycheck and that she was going to have to save up her money for a while before she could come on board. Here's what we all may need to agree on: a prospect that cannot come up with $300 to spend on something he or she really wants without bringing his or her lifestyle to a complete halt is not a prospect for you at this time. Chances are that this person, if he or she lives in America and is above the age of twenty–five (and especially if he or she is forty or older) has done a whole lot wrong financially and is probably not going to correct the bad financial decisions that he or she has been making any time soon.

Conventional wisdom says that people with financial problems tend to hang around and talk to other people with bad financial problems on a regular basis, and people flush with money that tend to make great financial decisions typically hang around and talk on a regular basis with other people who make great financial decisions. In my nearly thirty years of involvement in the network marketing industry, I have also found that when I show up at the home of someone who has joined us in business to do their BOP, that person often has guests who are in similar financial situations.

Therefore, if my host is in great financial condition and is flush with money; his or her guests also tend to be. Conversely, if my host is in a bad financial situation, and has been for some time, his or her guests tend to be in the same situation. The exception to this is the very–well–to–do family member who always makes great financial decisions, is flush with money, and is constantly trying to drag his or her friends or family members across the financial finish line to no avail.

This is how these scenarios sometimes play out: you show up at your new team member's home to do a BOP, and this person has a house full of people because he or she is held in very high regard by many. So you might think this will be a great sign–up day for distributors and customers for this new rep, because the guests trust the financial decision making of the host. But then it starts to come out that if these relatives and friends are going to join the business, they are going to have to depend on the well–to–do host (who is their friend or relative) to pay their way into the business. Typically, these well–intentioned team members will tell you that they invited these particular guests because they want to get these family members and friends going in a business of their own so that they too can enjoy the fruits of financial independence.

You will now need to educate your well–to–do new team member about the fact that people have certain tendencies. As one of my good buddies, Jerry Konohia, once said to me, and I paraphrase, "People who make a lot of money have a tendency to hang around people who make a lot of money, and thus they tend to make even more money together. Conversely, people who have a tendency to stay in financial trouble have a tendency to hang around other people who tend to stay in financial trouble, and they have a tendency to keep losing money together." So you have to help your new team member understand that it is going to be a whole lot more profitable and productive for you to help him or her to build the business by working with his or her financially well-off friends and associates first. Then, after he or she is having financial success in the business, that may be the time to help those family members who are going to want him or her to pay their way into the business.

I know these can be harsh words, but I don't want you to get burned out before you become wealthy in this business. Are there exceptions to the rule? Of course there are, but I would rather you, initially at least, focus your limited time and energy working with prospects that fit the rule rather than waiting for that rare person who is the exception to the rule.

With that said, if you plan to become successful in the network marketing industry, one of the first things you must do is make a list of possible prospects, preferably two hundred to five hundred people right out of your e-mail or mobile phone lists. Then separate these people into two categories: those you are pretty sure don't have financial problems and those you are pretty sure constantly do have financial problems. Build first with the ones who do not have any financial problems, and have them do the same. After you have become financially successful in your new network marketing business, then you can come back to the people on your lists that typically do have financial problems.

Why is focusing first on your better-off prospects so important? This is important because someone has to win. You have to win in order to be that motivating force to those who are standing by and waiting to say, "See, I told you that network marketing stuff doesn't work. But oh, by the way, can I borrow some money?" Just thought I'd add a little levity there.

Keys to Success

- Know your Why.
- Set a small goal.
- Personality matters.
- High energy equals high income.
- Learn and understand the compensation plan and follow the system.
- Go to the people you know who have money.
- Become a product of the product.
- Always recruit.
- Stay plugged in.
- NEVER QUIT.

CHAPTER 5

Choosy Lover

How Do I Choose a Company to Love?

- Research.
- Narrow it down to two companies.
- Ensure that the company produces a marketable product that you can sell.
- Find a mentor.

Research

You can search the Web to find out just about anything about everything. Make the Internet your first stop, but not your only source of research, as some information may not be completely trustworthy or accurate. It is essential to get first–hand accounts of network marketing businesses from people who have actually made some good money in them (good money being whatever income number floats your boat). Take the comments "that stuff doesn't work" with a grain of salt.

Some people fail at this business, just as some people can't successfully run a McDonald's franchise. Network marketing businesses, just like any computer company, beauty salon, or shoe store, can and do go out of business from time to time. So, is it possible to run into a person who had a bad experience while working with a network marketing company? Sure. This person may have been very optimistic about the financial success that he or she wanted to achieve with that company, but something unforeseen happened, and that company went out of business. However, typically what I've found is that people who lament about a company not working out for them may be reluctant to say what really happened, which was possibly that they paid their sign-up fee and then expected money to magically flow to them with very little effort on their part.

What happens to all people who join a networking marketing company is that they quickly realize that to become financially successful with that company, they are going to have to really go to work. That company, figuratively speaking, may grow overalls, a hard hat, and some steel toe boots, and may take more work than they are willing to put into it. Some people set out to become entrepreneurs until they realize how much work becoming an entrepreneur really takes. I will say that if you focus for a short period on building your business, say three to six years, you will be able to set yourself up for financial freedom. I always like to say that 'if you will focus and work on your business for 36 months the way others will not, then you will be able to live for the next 36 years and beyond in a way that others can only dream of.

Most people have never sold anything in their lives (independent of an employer that is). They don't necessarily understand that in direct sales, people invest and believe in you before they make a buying decision about the product or service that you are marketing to them. Therefore, if you haven't taken time to prepare a well-crafted presentation or to learn the ins and outs of your products, your prospects may reject you—not because they don't like the product, but because they may sense that you have not taken the time to become knowledgeable.

You don't have to become an expert—just take the time to at least become knowledgeable about your products. Ensure that the product is something marketable that you can sell. Make sure it is something that you care about or can get excited about. Don't try to sell something you don't like. Have an understanding of the use and value of the product, especially if the product is something that you never used prior to joining this company.

My mentors in the industry always trained me to understand that you have to become a user of the products or services that you are selling if you are going to really have a shot at being successful with a particular company. Sometimes you can make people believe that you know about a product or service that you don't use yourself, but it is a lot more productive to build your team and your business with a company that sells products you actually use and like. Now, this doesn't mean that you have to use every product that the company markets, but find something in the portfolio of products that you can get excited about and be able to give a personal testimony about.

Narrow It Down to Two Companies

There are hundreds of network marketing companies for you to choose from when you begin or continue in your network marketing career. Be proactive in your search, ask friends and family members if they know of anyone who has made money in the network marketing industry, and then ask them to introduce you to these successful entrepreneurs. Interview these people and ask them lots of questions. Ask them what made them choose the company they are with. Ask them how their compensation plan works.

Find out what's so special about their products or services. After a while, you will get used to the vocabulary and the industry jargon; this will help you make company evaluations more quickly. Narrow down your choice of companies to two companies; then have the uplines of those two companies really let you know why choosing to join their team is going to be the best choice for you. My mentors in the industry always trained me that you have to become a user of the products or services that you are selling if you are going to really have a shot at being successful with a particular company.

Sometimes you can make people believe that you know about a product or service that you don't use yourself, but it is a lot simpler to build your team and your business with a company that sells products you actually use and like. Now, this doesn't mean that you have to use every product that the company markets but find something in the portfolio of products that you can get excited about and be able to give a personal testimony about.

Find a Mentor

Find someone you can trust. Find someone who wants you to succeed. Put your mentor in the position of benefiting from your success. Don't expect him or her to carry you. Recognize that your mentor is doing you a favor. Always have plenty of good questions.

Feel prospective mentors out—the relationship between a mentor and a mentee is like a marriage (but potentially much more lucrative). It is okay (to extend the metaphor) to go on a few dates before you move in together. When you find someone you like, someone you communicate well with, then pounce. Get on board. Hitch your wagon to that horse. (I mixed metaphors: you should never marry a horse.)

Get comfortable with your mentor. Take lots of notes. You will frequently need to refer back to your notes because your upline will be busy, and they won't always be available to answer your questions. Also, you may want to be thinking ahead to that time when you will need to be the mentor to your downline.

I say once again, pick someone you believe you can trust and a person that you feel genuinely cares about your ability to win. Now, this next one is a very critical step, be sure to ask politely, but be sure to ask to visually scan his or her last three months of pay stubs from the business. Also ask them if they are being paid any compensation from the company outside of the compensation plan. If the person refuses to show you those pay stubs, or says that it is against their company's policy to show you their checks, walk away, as those are usually red flags. Think about it: would you accept a job and begin working at that job prior to knowing when, how, and how much you were going to get paid? This is a critical step that you must take seriously because network marketing can make you a liar.

Here's what I mean: often you have people and companies who may publish some big checks that some of their top distributors have earned. However, sometimes those large checks may not have been due to regular monthly activity from their teams but due to a short term promotion. Therefore, distributors may not receive such large commission checks every month.

However, some distributors and companies may try to lead you to believe that this distributor earns this amount of money every month. They may believe that such actions are good for recruiting, when it's actually just lying to people. I'm sure that some of the more experienced network marketers reading this book can attest to what I am saying.

Most often, that's not the distributor's goal, to become a liar, but many people will do it when they see other leaders in the company doing the same thing. Find a sponsor/mentor who doesn't mind showing you his or her checks. You want to work with someone who is skilled, capable, and patient enough to work with you. This doesn't mean that you get to eat up all of your mentor's time. You should try your best to prove that you are an asset to his or her team as quickly as possible. If your mentor sets limits, such as when you can call him or her, abide by those limits. Fantastic mentors need sleep, too.

Other Tips:

- Pick a product that you feel strongly about.
- Pick a product that people inherently need.
- Pick a reputable company.
- Develop a keen awareness of what is or isn't a scam.
- Pick an untapped market.

CHAPTER 6

Compensation Plans Explained

Understanding Compensation Plans

This chapter should get your heart racing. It should have your full and undivided attention. This is the chapter that will help you manifest all the wonderful dreams that you and your new team members will write into your dream books. Those dreams you have that some friends, family members, or even co-workers tell you that you will never achieve. You are going to prove them all wrong and then turn around and help them to achieve the same success. You have to believe that you were put here to *live* your making and not just to make a *living*!

Your compensation plan will determine how and when you get paid. The goal is to earn enough money in the business so that it will pay for all those wonderful dreams and grand experiences that may not have come about if you could only depend on the salary from your job to pay for them. Therefore, it makes sense that you should intimately understand how the plan works, right? Again, would you accept a job and begin working at that job prior to knowing when, how, and how much you were going to get paid? I didn't think so. Just bear with me—compensation plans look complicated at first, but I will walk you through the basics.

At the conclusion of this chapter, you should understand the five basic compensation plan structures and how they work. This chapter will also evaluate the benefits and limitations of each of these compensation plans. This way you can decide for yourself which one is the best for you.

Questions to Ask:

- Are you being paid for one–on–one demonstrations?
- Are you being paid when new distributors sign up?
- Do you get a percentage of your team's commissions?
- Do you get a bonus for team members' recruits?
- Do you receive a commission for your teams' customers' monthly recurring orders?
- Is there a car bonus (a car that you can win or earn)?
- Is there a company–sponsored trip (a common form of bonus for top performers)?

Here are the five basic compensation plan structures:

- unilevel plan
- stair–step breakaway plan
- forced matrix plan
- binary plan
- combination or hybrid plan

How to Understand a Compensation Plan
Every network marketing company's compensation plan is different, but they are all based around one of these five structures. The

numbers may shift and the vocabulary might change, but fear not: you can make them all very simple to work with. The difference between compensation plans that use the same or similar structures is the base commission and the additional bonuses that each company may add. To understand any compensation plan completely, you need to first understand some basic concepts and vocabulary used by people in the network marketing industry. Most of these definitions are adapted from those given in the article "Compensation Plan, Part II" on Fernando Cortez's blog.[14]

Sponsor

Your sponsor is the person responsible for introducing you to the business. You signed up with his or her network marketing company. Your sponsor is also the person responsible for making sure that you receive adequate training and support.[15]

Distributor or Associate

This is what you are. Companies use these two words interchangeably. There are others, but these are the two most common terms.

Business Center

When you first join a network marketing company, you are given what we call a business center. Just think of the business center as your home—a place from which all your family members

---

14   Fernando Cortes, "Compensation Plan, Part II," How to Succeed in MLM without Losing Money (blog), July 1, 2014, http://www.mlmnetworkmarketingblog.com/compensation–plan–part–ii/

15   Most of these definitions are adapted from those given in the article "Compensation Plan, Part II" on Fernando Cortez's blog. Fernando Cortes, "Compensation Plan, Part II," How to Succeed in MLM without Losing Money (blog), July 1, 2014, http://www.mlmnetworkmarketingblog.com/compensation–plan–part–ii/#comment–2570.

originated, and a place that entitles you to get paid a commission for the volume or revenue that your organization (family) produces on a weekly, biweekly, or monthly basis (depending on what pay cycle your company chooses to use). The organization refers to both you and all the members (distributors) that you and your team have sponsored.

Think of your organization as a mall in which all the shops inside are independently owned and operated. Although you are not the boss of each shop (because each one is independently owned and operated), you do earn a profit from each of those stores' sales. In network marketing, as in any other business, the more productive your organization is, the more you get paid in return.

Upline/Downline

Two of the most common terms used in network marketing are upline and downline.[16]

Upline refers to all the individual distributor(s) who preceded you into the business and who share the same sponsor lineage. Although upline distributors should provide training and support to the members of their organization and help them become successful, their individual sponsoring efforts will normally have little or no impact on your commission check.

Downline refers to the individuals whom you have recruited and signed up as distributors into the business— your distributors recruits, their recruits and so forth and so on. You should always support your downline distributors. Though each member of your downline owns and operates his or her organization independently, the compensation plans typically are set up so that you get paid a portion of each of your downlines' commissions, so the more they make, the more you make. It's a win–win situation.

---

16 Ibid.

Level

Level refers to the position of a distributor in a downline relative to an upline distributor. Basically, anyone you recruit will be a level below you. Anyone they recruit will be two levels below you, and so on.

Width and Depth[17]

One of the main differences between the numerous compensation plan structures is the width and depth of the plan.

Width refers to the maximum number of distributors who you can have placed immediately under you in the compensation structure. This is commonly known as your frontline.[18]

"Depth" refers to the number of levels in which you can earn a commission on your distributors' sales.[19]

There are only so many times you can split a dollar, so a commission based on the work of downline distributors can only go so deep. In a forced matrix structure, the width and depth of the plan is normally written as a simple equation (width x depth).

In some compensation structures, it is possible to have infinite width (unilevel and stair–step breakaway plans), while other plans may have unlimited depth (such as a binary plan). Each plan will be discussed in more detail later.

Crossline

Crossline refers to the relationship between two or more distributors who work for the same company—all distributors on the same level would be crossline from one another. Typically, crossline does not factor into distributors' commissions.[20]

---

17 Ibid.
18 Ibid.
19 Ibid.
20 Ibid.

Legs

Every frontline distributor that you sponsor into your organization forms a new leg. These are the people that they recruit, creating levels under you.[21]

Point Value

Every industry has the same goal, which is to sell a product or service in high volume. Network marketing is no different. For every product sold in network marketing, a predetermined amount of the profit is paid to the team of distributors who were responsible for the sale.

The easiest and fairest way to pay a distributor's commission is to use a point system. Each product has an assigned point value, and your commission is determined by the volume of points that flow through your organization.[22]

This way, it doesn't matter where you operate your business from (e.g., America, Australia, Japan, etc.)—you are entitled to the same commission that any of your colleagues would receive anywhere in the world. It is important to understand that although higher–priced products normally offer a higher point value as a reward, this is not always the case.

One advantage of the point system is that because different products have different point values, if a company is trying to promote a particular product, it can allocate a higher point value to the product as an incentive for distributors to sell that product.[23]

---

21 Ibid.

22 Ibid.

23 Ibid.

The table below summarizes an example of point values.

Product	Price	Point Value
X	$20.00	$15
Y	$10.00	$10
Z	$25.00	$16

Calculating Points and Commissions

The commission you earn in a network marketing business is directly related to the total number of points (sales) that you accrue. Your goal is to build your business so that you have a greater number of points flowing through your organization, earning you a higher commission check.

Each compensation plan structure calculates points (sales) in a slightly different way, but plans normally take into account these variables:

- **Level volume:** the number of points (sales) that each level of your business has accumulated in that pay period.
- **Leg volume:** the number of points (sales) that each leg of your business has accumulated in that pay period.[24]
- **Group volume:** the number of points (sales) that have accumulated through your entire organization in that pay period.[25]
- **Carry–over volume:** the number of points (sales) you were not paid a commission on in your last pay period that is then carried over to the next pay period. You are then

---

24 Ibid.

25 Ibid.

entitled to earn a commission on these sales in your next pay period. Carry–over volume basically allows any unpaid points (sales) to carry over to the following pay period so that you don't lose any commission.[26]

Variable Level Commissions

This is where compensation plans can become confusing, both for people who may be looking at this type of business for the first time and for some experienced distributors. In particular, the stair–step breakaway, unilevel, and forced matrix plans normally offer a variable commission rate for each level of the distributors within your organization. All this really means is that the plans offer different percentages based on your position relative to your downline.[27]

For example, if you had a variable commission rate, you could receive a ten percent commission based on your first–level team's volume and production, a 15 percent commission based on your second–level team's volume and production, and another five percent commission based on your third level team's volume and production. Alternatively, if the compensation plan offered a consistent commission rate, then you would earn the same commission percentage for each level (e.g., ten percent for all three levels).[28]

What Is the Best Plan?

Every compensation plan has its upsides and downsides, some of which are discussed below. When it comes to picking the best plan, it really depends on what your needs are and what sounds the most reasonable to you. Typically it's not just the pay plan that will motivate you to join and build a team with a particular company. Often

---

26 Ibid.

27 Ibid.

28 Ibid.

it's a combination of the relationship that the prospect has with the person who is attempting to recruit him or her into the business, the company's compensation plan, and the product mix that will usually inform the prospect's final decision on which company to join and build with. However, since this is a relationship business, it is not unusual for a person to join a business solely based on the relationship that the recruiter has with the prospect.

The Unilevel Plan

The unilevel plan has been around for many years and is still used by a number of network marketing companies today. The main benefit to this model is that it is very easy to understand. However, as is the case with all compensation plans, there are benefits and drawbacks that should be considered.

Unilevel plans only enable you to sponsor one line of distributors; therefore, everyone you sponsor is on your frontline. There are no width limitations to this plan, which means that there is no limit to the number of people you can sponsor in your frontline. Commissions are normally paid out on a limited depth. The goal of this plan is to recruit a large number of frontline distributors and then encourage them to do the same.

To earn a commission using this structure typically involves a minimal number of personal sales. This makes it easier for part–timers to earn an income. Though it tends to be easier to earn a commission using a unilevel compensation structure, the commissions are typically smaller than those of other compensation plans. This means that your primary revenue stream will be from recruiting distributors unless the company modifies the compensation plan to pay a lot more for selling products directly to customers, which many companies have done these days.

One of the main disadvantages of the plan is that every distributor you sponsor becomes crossline to all your other frontline distributors, and they must then work in competition with one another. This can present numerous challenges for newcomers who try to recruit friends and family into their business, because essentially they will be working in competition to one another. An ever-increasing frontline means that you will constantly be training and managing large groups of people.

The unilevel plan does, however, have a few advantages. The main advantage is that it is easy to explain. Generally, the more distributors you recruit, the larger your commissions check. This makes it attractive to your experienced network marketers, particularly those who are top-gun recruiters and have the ability to develop management and training systems for their growing downline.

Given the competition created between frontline distributors within this compensation structure, it is common for distributors operating with this compensation plan to target their cold market (people they don't know) as a way to build their organization. This may include developing lead-generation systems and the use of Internet leads or using the old-fashioned strategy of walking up to a stranger in a grocery store and starting up a conversation.

Most modern network marketing companies using this model have made slight changes to its basic structure to make it more attractive and allow some teamwork to take place. Additionally, most unilevel plans now also include a number of bonuses to make their compensation plan more appealing. Another advantage of modern-day unilevel plans is that when distributors rank advance (get promoted to a higher payout level), they are generally entitled to earn a higher commission rate on their team's volume and production as well.

This compensation model is generally best suited for those who have network marketing experience or those who are very confident in their ability to recruit and train a large number of frontline distributors. Like most compensation structures, this model does offer the potential to earn a very high income if you are willing to put in the work. However, as discussed previously, I strongly encourage you to avoid joining a network marketing company based on its compensation plan alone.[29]

The Stair–Step Breakaway Plan

The stair–step breakaway plan was one of the original network marketing compensation plans and is still used by a number of companies today. (Please see exhibit 9, which features an excel document detailing my experience with a stair–step breakaway plan and shows how we received our organizational genealogy reports prior to the advances of currently used software.) Since this structure has been around for many years and has a proven track record, it is frequently implemented by start–ups; however, as with all compensation plan structures, it has both some advantages and a number of disadvantages. The name stair–step breakaway is derived from the concept that distributors climb the ladder of success, and when they reach a certain level; they are allowed to break away from their upline distributors and run their organizations independently.

As distributors break away from their upline, this allows them to earn a greater commission on their downlines' new recruits. As you can see in exhibit 9 (on the right side of the page), there are titles and names under those titles: AR = Area Rep, SR = Senior Rep, RD = Regional Director, SD = Senior Director. These are the levels that you will ascend to as your organization grows, or the breakaways, which are also called codes. So those of us in the business might say, "Steve is in my AR and SR code, but he is in Bob's RD and ED codes." This also determines who gets the bonus money. Let's say that the AR = $100, SR = $75, RD = $50, ED = $25, and SD = $15, so the bonuses equal a total of $265 that will be paid out on every distributor who comes into your organization.

---

29 Ibid.

So if I brought the person into the business—and as you see in exhibit 9, the AR code has my name under it, Moats—I would qualify to receive the $100 bonus, but the remaining $165 would be paid out to my upline leaders. Fields was the SR, so he would receive the $75; Fields was also the RD, so he would therefore also receive $50. Orberson was the ED—he would receive the $25. The $15 was not paid out in this instance because no one had yet qualified to become an SD.

Your goal—the motivating carrot of the plan—is for you to build your organization and get promoted to the higher levels so that one day the entire $265 bonus paid out on every distributor is coming to you. You can see an example of this in exhibit 10, which shows that I was now receiving the AR, SR, RD, and ED payout ($250) — since no one had yet reached SD, that $15 had yet to be paid out.

Now, this bonus payout gets sexy when you have scores or even hundreds of people coming into each code. For example, let's say that this month you were qualified to receive the bonuses all the way up to ED, and let's say that you had ten people come into your AR code. Those ten people x $100 = $1,000; forty people coming into your SR code x $75 = $3,000; thirty people coming into your RD code x $50 = $1,500; and fifty–five people coming into your ED code x $25 = $1,375. That adds up to a total bonus payout to you that month of $6,875. Whether you accomplished this as a full time or part time distributor, that bonus payout may not be too shabby, depending on your expectations.

When a company is in its hyper–growth or momentum phase, lots of distributors are beginning to notice and join the company. This can then propel them into reaching a critical mass (the point in time when tons of distributors are joining your company each month and everyone is finding it very easy to earn big checks). In this phase, the distributors with very large teams may have thousands of distributors coming into each code each month, and that's when you see the checks that we all live for in the business. People may make $200,000, $300,000, or even $400,000 per month.

The stair–step breakaway plan resembles the unilevel plan in that each distributor is only allowed to sponsor one level of distributors (frontline). While there is no limit to the width (number of frontline distributors) that you can sponsor, the stair–step breakaway plan offers limited incentive for teamwork within your organization, and the competition between crossline distributors can make it difficult to recruit close friends and family into this structure.

As with all network marketing companies, the main goal for each business associate is to market and then build a team that markets the company's products or services. This is achieved in the stair–step breakaway plan by recruiting as many frontline distributors as you can, just as with the unilevel compensation plan. The primary difference between the unilevel compensation plan and the stair–step breakaway compensation plan is "the breakaway."

The Breakaway

Breaking away from your upline has numerous benefits to the individual distributor, including earning a higher commission rate. But it can have a seriously negative impact on the organization that you break away from. When you break away, the volume that your upline leader previously received from your team no longer flows through you and up to him or her at the same rate. For your upline, it is like losing one of their best customers. As distributors break away, the original sponsor is still entitled to earn a small percentage from each breakaway distributor's efforts. This is referred to as an override commission. Each breakaway organization is referred to as a generation, and although distributors are entitled to earn an override commission on all their breakaway generations, this override commission is only a small fraction in comparison to the commissions they were earning previously.

Another drawback with the stair–step breakaway plan is that you are not the only person entitled to break away. On the plus side, once you reach the level where you are allowed to break away from your upline, you will earn a larger commission on your team. On the minus side, if you are serious about building your team, then one day your team will grow large enough that distributors in your downline may also qualify to break away from you. Although initially having a distributor break away from your organization can put a dent in your short–term income, creating a number of breakaway organizations can help you to earn a long–term residual income from the generational bonuses to be paid out. It can also serve to refocus your time toward developing a frontline of future leaders.

In general, this plan is most suited to those distributors who are confident in their ability to recruit new distributors and who have good management skills. For those looking at this compensation plan for the first time, one thing to consider is that you may experience a lack of support from your upline once you are established, and you will be working in competition with other crossline distributors. While the potential commissions can be very rewarding with this compensation structure, the binary plan and the matrix plan are generally considered more friendly and supportive for newcomers.

In the past, some companies who used the stair–step breakaway gave the industry a bad name. In these particular companies, the group sales volume (GSV) was set at unrealistic targets, and new distributors were encouraged to purchase extra product to assist their upline to earn a commission. Consequently, a lot of distributors ended up being stuck with stock they could not sell. High hopes were drummed into some of the distributors, leading them into financial trouble. Fortunately, to my knowledge, this rarely happens today.

However, if it appears that the company you are analyzing is encouraging you and your new recruits to do this, I suggest you try a different company.

The stair–step breakaway plan can sometimes be a little more difficult for many people to understand, which means that it may be a little more challenging to try to explain to your prospective recruits. It was not until I reached a certain level of success with this plan and had enough content on my genealogy reports—allowing me to analyze the strong parts and the weak parts of the organization that I was building—that I thoroughly understood how this type of compensation plan worked.

The stair–step breakaway plan does have a number of advantages. It has a good track record, which makes it attractive to new companies looking for a proven business model. In particular, the stair–step breakaway plan works to benefit those distributors who have good selling or recruiting skills. Some might argue that this compensation plan is more suited to the full–timers; however, recent advancements in the industry, particularly the Internet, can make it just as friendly to the part–time distributor.[30]

The Matrix Plan

The matrix plan, also called the forced matrix plan, is based on a structure that has a set width and depth. Although there are many variations to this compensation plan, its basic structure is identified by a simple equation that distinguishes the width and depth of the plan (width x depth). For example, a 3 x 5 plan suggests you can only sponsor a maximum of three frontline distributors, and you have the potential to earn commissions up to five levels deep.

---

30 Ibid.

Since the width of this compensation structure is limited, distributors are encouraged to assist their downline members in order to grow their organizations. Any new recruits you sponsor after your frontline is full must be positioned under one of your existing downline distributors. This process is commonly referred to as spillover (this is also used in the binary plan). The main advantage of this concept is that it creates an element of teamwork in which distributors within your organization can work together and mutually benefit from one another.

The forced matrix structure allows distributors to sponsor new recruits deeper into their downline once their frontline is full. Traditionally, these new distributors were automatically placed into the next available frontline position; however, more recently, plans have been developed to allow distributors to decide where they want to position these new distributors. This recent modification has made this structure more appealing, as it gives distributors more control over their business and increases the amount of teamwork. One of the main advantages of the matrix plan over the unilevel plan and the stair–step breakaway plan is that once your frontline is full, your focus changes toward developing your frontline distributors and assisting them in finding and training their frontline distributors.

A downside of the matrix plan is that the commissions paid on each level are variable. There is more incentive for distributors to assist some levels of their downline but not others. Additionally, some plans are quite wide and require you to fill six or more frontline positions before assisting your frontline distributors to develop their organizations. Another drawback to the variable commission rate is that its incentives can be hard to explain to potential prospects. You could have the best company in the world, but if the compensation plan is too hard to explain, it could be very challenging to get others to join.

When reviewing compensation plans, in particular the different forced matrix structures, you should be aware that the narrower and deeper the plan, the more supportive your upline distributors will be. For example, a 2 x 12 plan encourages more teamwork and support from upline distributors than a 6 x 4 plan. That being said, you should also consider the variable commission rate, as some wider plans have an incentive for distributors to focus their efforts toward assisting different levels of distributors. To make forced matrix plans more attractive, some companies have added "infinity bonuses" and "roll-up compressions," allowing hardworking distributors to earn commissions on levels specified outside the depth of the plan.

In summary, the matrix compensation plans have the potential to be very rewarding to both newcomers and top-gun recruiters, particularly once you understand the compensation structure in its entirety. Like most compensation structures, this model does offer you the potential to earn a very high income if you are willing to put in the work.[31]

The Binary Plan

Even though the binary plan was only introduced in the '90s and is relatively new to the network marketing industry, it is already very popular among network marketing companies and members within the industry. In addition to the simplicity of the binary compensation structure, there are a number of advantages that make it attractive to all network marketers, including those new to the industry, part-timers, average networkers, and your more experienced top-gun recruiters.

How Does the Binary Compensation Plan Work?

The binary plan, as the name suggests, is based around the number two, which represents the maximum number of frontline associates

---

31   Ibid.

that any business center can have. Typically, you would place one of your personally sponsored distributors on your left side (hereafter called your left leg) of your business center and then another personally sponsored distributor on the right side of that business center (hereafter called your right leg). This is all done by you and your upline leader in the beginning when you start your business—your upline leader usually will guide you with your placement of distributors until you have gotten the hang of how to do it yourself, and sometimes your company customer service representative can do this for you as well.

This is all done via the software that is used by your company in the replicated website that most, if not all, companies provide their distributors today. Any additional distributors must then be placed under one of your existing frontline members. This creates a very supportive environment for new members, as the easiest way for associates to achieve success is to assist their new members to build their organizations. This team approach makes the binary plan very attractive, since it provides a lot of support (both initially and ongoing) for all the associates within your organization as they work toward achieving a common goal.

The main earning objective of the binary compensation plan is to balance the amount of leg volume flowing through either side of your business center. For example, if you have 800 sales points flowing through the left leg of your business (which means that at least $800 worth of product was sold by your team in that leg) but only 500 points flowing through the right, you are paid out on the highest common denominator. In this instance, that is 500 points from both sides. When the binary plan was first introduced, any additional volume (the extra 300 points on the left) would be lost (profit to the company in a practice called "Flushing"), making it difficult for part–timers to make serious money. However, most binary plans now allow any additional volume to be carried over (saved to be paid out in the future) to the following commission period. This "carry–over" feature has proven to be very popular for part–timers, because it means that you don't ever lose any of the sales volume that you have acquired.

The goal is to balance the sales volume flowing through your organization. This encourages associates to help their weaker downline members to build their organization (promoting team-work) to achieve a better volume balance and more consistent (and higher) commission checks. There are normally no depth re-strictions to the binary structure, and each level of your organiza-tion is paid out on a consistent commission percentage, making it easy to understand.

One of the main distinctions of the binary plan is that it is vol-ume driven as opposed to level driven, which means that you may not have to have as large an organization as you may have to have to be successful in some of the other types of compensation plans. This also means there is an incentive to help new associates in your organization, no matter how deep they are.

In fairness to good math, because there are no depth restric-tions to the binary plan, each business center has a limited earning potential, which maxes out to ensure that both distributors and the company earn a profit.

If each business center has a limit to how much it can earn, how is it possible to earn millions of dollars through a network market-ing business using the binary plan?

What makes the binary plan profitable for serious network marketers is that although each business center can only earn so much; there is generally no limit to how many business centers each distributor can operate. Think of a business center as a shop—if you currently own a shop that is doing very well but no longer has the potential to grow, what can you do? You can open a second shop, as this now allows you to earn profits from both shops. Well, you can expand your business in exactly the same way using the binary plan.

Once you have achieved a certain level with your network marketing business, and your organization has maxed out or has limited potential to earn you more money, the company usually allows the distributor to purchase a new business center. The company is happy because it has an experienced, successful distributor opening another business center, and the distributor is happy because now he or she has higher earning potential. The more business centers the distributor has that are generating volume and revenue, the greater the earning potential of the distributor. Take, for instance, exhibit 11, my Maxxis 2000 genealogy report—you will see that we were using a binary compensation plan. Exhibit 12 shows that the report was from April 2002, and the person who sponsored me into the business was R.J.S. Holdings. Exhibit 13 shows that I had multiple business centers, to include Damon Moats and DDM Group, and then I sponsored the rest of my team under those two business centers, which would both accumulate sales volume and pay out commissions to me.

The Binary Compensation Plan Helps Even the Average Network Marketer

Studies conducted into the network marketing industry have shown that the average network marketing distributor sponsors, on average, two to three new distributors into their businesses. This means that some of the older plans that could require you to personally sponsor forty to fifty distributors to be successful might not be as appealing today. These older plans started to give the industry a bad reputation as being "too hard"—fortunately, most of these plans have since been modified.

After these studies started to appear in the 1980s, the binary plan was created to give everybody a fair chance of success. Since the binary compensation structure only allows the sponsoring of two frontline distributors to each business center, even your less-than-average network marketer still has the potential to achieve financial freedom using this compensation model. Additionally, the binary compensation plan was developed so that if you are a new recruit and you are really struggling to build your downline, it is in the interest of your upline distributors to give you as much help as they possibly can.

Take, for instance, exhibits 14 and 15, which are snapshots of my genealogy report from Ardyss International from December 2014 and show the first page of my team's 267–page genealogy report (middle of exhibit 15) with this company. It shows 50 distributors on each page, which equates to more than another 10,000 distributors (267 x 50 = 13,350, to be exact) that I, and my totally new team, had now put into a third company. The first large national team that I built was for Excel Telecommunications from 1995–1997, the next was for Maxxis 2000 from 1997–2001, and the most recent was for Ardyss International, from 2009–2010. I started in Ardyss International in May of 2009, as you can see in exhibit 16, which shows that after my first month, even though I had started recruiting, I had not yet received a check by the end of June 2009. But by the end of July, I had qualified to receive my first check, which was $1,325.21 (as you can see in exhibit 17). I was now a proud member of the comma club, which is a term that we use in the network marketing industry to describe people who are starting to make checks in the thousands—people who are starting to be perceived by their upline leaders as being a bit more serious about building their businesses than most people will be.

As you can see in exhibit 18, my next check, for September 2009, was $3,261.25. We were starting to gain momentum because some of the superstars that I had recruited back in May and June were starting to build their teams and purchase lots of products. In exhibit 19, you can see from the screenshot that my check for the end of November 2009 was $8,246.73, and exhibit 20 shows that in December 2009 my team produced $104,345.89 in group sales volume (GSV).

Moving forward, my best month with Ardyss International was April 2010; exhibit 21 shows that my check was $20,612.70, and exhibit 22 shows that my team produced $187,342.61 in GSV in April 2010. But this is where the wheels came off the company. As you will see going forward, my team continued to grow, and in October 2010 we produced $643,314.89 in one month—yet again my team and I had built another multi–multimillion dollar revenue sales organization.

Unfortunately, the company decided to cut the compensation plan that my team and I had been recruited with in May 2009. Under this plan, we were to be paid additional bonus money monthly (this became a permanent expectation of the compensation plan) when the company activated a promotion called double points. Double points simply meant that if your team produced $40,000 in sales that month, the company would pay you at the level of $80,000 that month, as long as this sales volume was properly distributed throughout your organization. If you qualified for this bonus, you were then thrust into a higher payout level. This bonus is what fueled the company's expedient growth. Once it was taken away, most leaders' incomes began to evaporate rapidly.

This change was devastating. The effects were what you would expect to see if you were in the following situation. Imagine that you were hired by a company with the knowledge and assumption that the pay that you were receiving when you started that job was the pay that you would continue to receive as long as you worked with that company.

Then, one day, your employer called you into the office or sent you an e-mail stating that you could continue to work for the company but that your pay would be cut by anywhere from 70 to 80 percent. How would you feel? That's what happened to my team—the more than 10,000 distributors who were my business partners and the tens of thousands of other distributors in the company domestically and internationally who were enjoying great paydays for doing their job, which was building their businesses.

Exhibit 22 illustrates what happened as my team around the world (because we had now built a team that included great leaders domestically and in other great countries like Nigeria and England) got wind of the pay cut. When the company announced that it was no longer going to pay us based on the double points, which I was told started out as a promotion a year earlier, but by the time I came on-board in 2009 the company was marketing it as a permanent part of the compensation plan, the team momentum and GSV (group sales volume) slowed substantially, and almost everyone's business centers became unbalanced as most people were now quitting the business because the compensation plan was abysmal without double points. My check for December 2010 dropped back down to only $1,707.35, which you can see in exhibit 23. My team and I went off looking for a new company to build wealth with. [32]

In my network marketing career, I had now been a part of a company, Maxxis 2000, which was full of fraudulent activity from the owner. Because of that experience, I thought I knew how to read the tea leaves about things to come. Unfortunately, within six months of joining Ardyss International, again lies told to me

---

32 Fernando Cortes, "Compensation Plan, Part II," How to Succeed in MLM without Losing Money (blog), July 1, 2014, http://www.mlmnetworkmarketingblog.com/compensation-plan-part-ii/#comment-2570.

and to other distributors around the country by Ardyss' owners about the alleged improvements they were making to their binary compensation plan, and also the ruse that we would be able to purchase pre-IPO shares of stock in the company, (ala Maxxis which you know had me raising my brow) I again became a whistle-blower, explaining to anyone that called me to ask me why their incomes were dropping precipitously that I was now seeing the same lies from Ardyss that I had heard from Maxxis a decade earlier.

Ardyss' owners had even flown to Maryland from Las Vegas, specifically to meet with me and my business partner Sharon Page, to promise us that they were going to get a proper compensation plan implemented very soon. Sadly, they did not and unfortunately I was right again. I so desperately wish I were wrong, and so did the five or six top distributors who had become my friends because I was trying to follow in their footsteps with this company, whose incomes had gone up to $100,000.00, yes one hundred thousand dollars or more monthly by the end of 2009 in Ardyss, but by the end of 2010, due to the many lies told by the owners about the compensation plan, many of their incomes had dropped to less than $5000 per month. They too left to join other companies.

Combination or Hybrid Plan

A combination or hybrid plan is a compensation plan that combines some aspects of the four aforementioned compensation plans. It may be a plan that combines a binary with a unilevel plan, a unilevel plan with a breakaway, or a matrix combined with a unilevel plan, for example. Usually the goal of a combination or hybrid compensation plan is to take the most desirable parts of a plan and combine it with the most desirable parts of another plan. This is done to appeal to distributors who have worked various plans and determined that some aspects of certain plans worked well for them but that some other aspects of the plan were less desirable.

CHAPTER 7

Attitude Determines Altitude

'm sure you were paying attention to the previous chapter on compensation plans and, therefore, you will see that the key to your success is your downline. This is not negotiable. There is no maybe in this. Your first priority should always be recruiting individuals who are as hungry to succeed as you are, or better yet, those who are actually more skilled and talented than you are.

You can get by recruiting randomly, but you may never see anything that looks like financial success. If there is any secret sauce that I may have in my recruiting efforts, it is that I try to recruit up as often as possible. This usually means going after the person who I feel is much more successful and talented than I am.

Start Reading Business Magazines

If you want to walk the walk, you have to talk the talk. You need to be well informed about business and management trends. You should know what is going on with business in general. People prefer to work with well-informed, business-savvy individuals. Read Forbes, Fortune, and other business magazines or blogs that will help you understand business and that therefore will help you understand and appreciate the power and the money in the network marketing industry.

Network marketing is an alternative to selling goods and services through a traditional brick-and-mortar store. In traditional store-front businesses, you usually have to spend a lot of money on advertising to get people into your establishment. Network marketing businesses have the same sales goals as any other business; however, rather than paying for advertising prior to a sale being made, network marketing companies pay the distributor a commission after the sale is made, via word of mouth advertising. This in effect reduces the amount of up-front capital needed to launch and sustain the company.

Buying low and selling high or even higher are the goals of every business. Some people have asked me whether having a traditional storefront is better than owning a network marketing company or distributorship, and my reply is, sometimes, but not always. Both models have their strengths and weaknesses. Again, a large part of your decision as to which model will work for you depends on your determination of how much money it will take for you to get the business off the ground. If your financial situation is anything like mine was when I decided I wanted to become an entrepreneur, the low entry cost of network marketing made it very appealing. Your mentor should be able to help you process the question of which model works best for you in your particular situation.

Having a Good Presentation Is Key

Becoming a good presenter with a good presentation comes with practice, practice, practice. I cannot over dramatize the importance of a powerful presentation. Your skill and personality will shine through in this moment and hopefully captivate your prospects. You cannot entice (in a good way) and properly inform your prospects about the great opportunity that exists within your company if you are unfamiliar with the content in your own presentation. You should speak in a rich, confident voice—not too booming and certainly not too muted. You must project confidence. Having a strong knowledge of the information in your presentation will significantly increase your overall confidence in your ability to build your team.

One of the training strategies that I have employed is that I frequently use one of my handheld devices to film myself doing presentations so that I can review the video later to judge the quality of my presentation. Often I also send the video files to my business partners so that they can judge and critique the quality of my presentations. I always find this exercise invaluable—some people may express to me, for example, that I was moving my hands too much or not making enough eye contact during the presentation. With video, I can see that for myself and make the necessary improvements, should I agree with them. It may be a little awkward or scary to watch yourself doing a presentation for the first time, but you really should do this at least once.

Action Step

As a matter of fact, I really would like you to stop reading the book at this point, pick up one of your mobile devices, and either film yourself or have someone else video you doing a brief presentation for just two minutes. When you review the video, take notes about any gestures and mannerisms that may appear odd or show that you may not be comfortable doing presentations—try to smooth those things out as best you can. But better yet, I want you to note the great things you did in the presentation that make you the rock star that you are.

I'm sure you are probably better at doing presentations than you thought you were. Practicing and having someone critique your presentations will speed up the time it will take you to become what we call, in the industry, a front–of–the–room presenter. Reaching this level is important because the secret to this business is that the person in front of the room doing all the presentations tends to be the person who is making the big money!

As you will see when you are a part of a network marketing company, the team that grows rapidly is the team that constantly trains its new distributors on how to become front–of–the–room presenters—everyone on this kind of team tends to make more money. Sometimes when I explain to distributors how making money in network marketing really works, they stop having me do their presentations for them—they suddenly develop the courage to do their own and their team's presentations themselves, even if they had to read the presentation script in front of prospects until they had it memorized.

With just a little more practice you too will become a jump–in–front–of–the–moving–bus high quality presenter. You want to become so good that everyone on your team wants you to do their presentations. This is critical because your team will mimic you, the leader. If you are feeling a sense of trepidation about doing presentations, which is the only way to build a team quickly, then your team members will also be hesitant to jump out there and do the company presentations at will, and little to no money will be made by any of the people involved.

Develop Financial Literacy

Success will come (in large part) from knowing where your money is coming from and what it is that you plan to do with your money. Do what you can to better understand your brokerage accounts and their associated interest rates as well as your various investments and their associated tax liabilities—you will eventually use this information as a part of your presentation. You will not be giving tax advice, but instead, you'll be sharing with prospects the financial benefits you have experienced due to owning your network marketing business.

Now, keep in mind that I am not a tax professional, nor do I want you to try to become one either. I simply give word–of–mouth advice that I received from my tax professional as it relates to my tax benefits since I now own a network marketing distributorship. I then ask my prospects to consult with their tax professionals as to what the tax benefits could be for them if they owned a network marketing distributorship as well. I even carry around with me a quick–reference guide of applicable tax deductions that I read in a book about the tax benefits of owning a business.

For months, I carried this guide around to make myself aware of how many things in my day–to–day life I could claim as tax deductions, as long as I was building my business while carrying out these activities. It has saved me a lot of money to date. Then I realized that many of the deductions that you can take advantage of are right on the Schedule C form from the IRS. Make the IRS your wealth–creation partner by getting your team to carry around a Schedule C form. It will remind them every day of the things they can write off on their taxes at the end of the year if they build their businesses and keep good records of their business–related activities and the associated transactions.

Unfortunately, many people do not keep accurate records of their business–related expenses that would make it more efficient for them to itemize these expenses and deduct them from their tax liability at the end of the year. However, you and your team will be better at doing this after you all have read this book. I had to become informed about keeping more accurate records of my business expenses when I first got started. One of the best pieces of advice that I was given was to get an American Express card to use exclusively for business expenses. AMEX provides you with accurate monthly and annual expense statements that you can use at the end of the year to accurately track your business expenses and deduct them from your end–of–year tax liability.

Listen, many of the day–to–day expenses that you incur may be tax deductible. Be smart and view the IRS as your business partner.

Action Step

Please stop right now, go to the Web, and find a Schedule C form. Print it, laminate it, and carry it around with you at all times. Use it as another recruiting tool for those people who may be very dismayed with their tax liability at the end of the year from their jobs that report their W-2 earnings on a 1040 EZ form. You may be able to show them that having your new home–based business now allows you to deduct, as business expenses, things that you normally do anyway, such as drive, go out to restaurants, and take vacations.

You see, once you are in business and as long as you make at least $600 per year in income from growing your business, you will receive a 1099 from the company you are a distributor with. This $600 of earned income from your network marketing business says to the IRS that you are treating this business as a business and not as a hobby. To my knowledge, hobby expenses are not tax deductible.

CHAPTER 8

Prospecting

Define Your Network

Break your network into the following categories:

1. People who you know are business–minded.
2. People who you think might be business–minded.
3. People who you don't think are business–minded.
4. People who you know are not business–minded.

Most people who are starting out in network marketing will want to recruit people in categories three and four above—they think that these people are not involved with a business because they haven't found the right opportunity or have not been properly inspired. Fight that urge. Aim for the people who fit categories one and two above—these are the people who are most likely to see the inherent value in your opportunity. These people are prime candidates to become your business partners. Eventually you can approach the people who fit into category number three, although you should really spend some time feeling them out first to judge their capability and motivation to do what will have to be done to warrant you spending time to train and develop them into successful business builders. It helps to know for sure whether someone has a desire or interest to do the real work it will take to build his or her business.

Be conscientious. Some people are not good targets for recruiting, but they still may want to purchase your product—sell your products to them; every compensation plan pays you to have outside customers as well as to recruit distributors. It may not be as profitable up front as recruiting them, but down the road the residual income from those customers will provide you with a dependable stream of cash from month to month.

Read a Book on the Network Marketing Industry at Least Every Six Months

In any industry, it is important to continue learning, to stay aware of trends, and to refine and refresh your knowledge. This is especially true in this business. There are many excellent books that provide a lot of information to distributors. I recommend that all my team members read books such as *Your First Year in Network Marketing* by Mark and Rene Reid Yarnell, and *Wave 3: The New Era in Network Marketing* by Richard Poe, among many others.

Create and Expand the Proper Network

Befriend successful, intelligent individuals so you can bounce ideas off them. It is easier to have successful distributors if you recruit individuals who already have good financial habits and money–making strategies. An old adage says that you can estimate someone's income by looking at his or her ten closest friends, and it goes on to say that if your nine closest friends are broke, you will soon be the tenth. Like–minded people are usually attracted to one another. Wealthy, successful people enjoy each other's company. So it is likely that befriending a successful individual will greatly increase your list of successful prospects.

Yes, you may be a bit nervous and even feel a little intimidated hanging around people who are a lot more successful than you are, but fear not; that new skin will look good on you, too. Believe it or not, this means that the person you feel intimidated to be around, due to his or her level of success, will probably be the first person to write you the check to join you in business. This is because (a) they can, and (b) they most likely want to see you succeed as well. Talk to people who are already making money and have good money-making tendencies.

Key Steps in Prospecting:

1. Recruit up.
2. Focus on people who earn at least $75,000–$180,000.
3. Focus on motivated people.
4. Never stop prospecting.
5. Don't babysit adults.

Recruit Up

Recruit people who are more successful than you are. Your average income will be close to the average income of your ten closest friends. Talk to and associate with people who make more money than you do. If your goal is to be a millionaire, then surrounding yourself with nine close friends who are millionaires certainly gives you a greater chance of being the tenth in the bunch.

If you surround yourself with people who always seem to struggle financially, you may never get your business off the ground. That would be bad for you and for them, as people need others to succeed so that they can see that success is possible for them as well. Studies show that people who make less than

$30,000 annually typically don't have the disposable income to succeed in a network marketing business; conversely, many people who make $200,000 or more annually may think that they are too advanced for network marketing. The sweet spot for people you will be able to build a successful network marketing team with, income wise, can be found among those who earn between $75,000 and $180,000 annually. These people have the disposable income and usually the like–minded network to build a successful network marketing business. Overcome your fear of talking to successful people. You may feel intimidated, and that's okay; just work through it, and remember what Dr. Susan Jeffers always say's, "feel the fear and do it anyway."

Focus on People Who Make $75,000–$180,000

Become the type of person that you want to recruit. Dress well. Be positive. The people you attract will be those who feel they have the most in common with you. Be the type of person who attracts successful people. Don't set out to recruit financially unsuccessful people in the hopes that they may make you feel good about where you are financially, as you will see some others do. Financially unsuccessful people who are indifferent to financial success usually will cost you more than you profit. If someone is financially unsuccessful, see if he or she really possesses the desire to become financially successful.

If you have fallen on hard times but your tenacity and motivation are still at an all–time high, then you still have the potential for success in this industry. This is actually one of the best kinds of people that you can recruit—that person who was a superstar at one time, but has fallen on hard times due to some circumstance. I like to recruit this person because I can certainly relate to him or her, and I have found that once a person has tasted and experienced success, he or she has the muscle memory to get back to that place again.

It is important that you learn how to differentiate between people who have fallen on hard times but are destined to be super-stars again and people who are going through hard times and really don't have the intestinal fortitude to make the sacrifices it will require to win financially. You must also learn how to quickly determine which type of person you have just recruited because you are going to have to spend some of your resources to assist the person in reaching his or her financial goals. Both your money and your time are critical. You really don't want to find yourself too frequently in the position of providing recruits with too much of your time or your money. These are both resources that you may never see again, leaving you with little to no ROI (return on investment). Your job is to recruit, train, educate, and motivate your team members. Support is necessary, but recruiting individuals who cannot financially support building their businesses themselves could cause you to become doubtful and disillusioned, and we can't let that happen.

When you are recruiting distributors and a prospect has expressed a desire to join you and your team in the business, you should ask if he or she has an extra $2,000–$3,000 on hand. This may sound like an outrageous sum of money initially, especially if the first order you placed for product or your start-up kit was only $500 or so, but you must be (and teach prospects to be) real and pragmatic with expected expenses. You will need to explain the costs outside the first order or start-up kit. If someone is reluctant to invest in his or her own success, then why would you? Break down for your prospects where they should anticipate spending money.

Talk about associated expenses with your recruits. I have found that a large part of building a successful national and even international network marketing business is setting proper expectations for your new team members from the outset. Whether your new team members take your advice and purchase the items that you tell them will help them succeed is totally up to them, because it's their business. However, if they don't purchase the recommended marketing materials up front, they are going to tend to recruit others who won't have the necessary materials to succeed, and usually that team will just dry up and wither away with no one achieving financial success.

Anticipated Start–Up Costs Could Include:

- $500 for the initial order
- $100 for business cards
- $200 for marketing materials
- $200 for additional products
- $100–$150 for gas
- $240 for a month's worth of business lunches

Recruits should have the capital for the start–up costs prior to collecting their first check. Their first check may never come if they don't have the means and resources to generate it.

Focus on Motivated People

Network marketing is a lot of hard work. It takes a lot of energy and effort to succeed at it. You want to find and recruit individuals who are focused, motivated, and passionate. These people will form a strong downline for you and for themselves. These people will not get frustrated easily, and they certainly won't call you every Monday morning at 8:00 a.m. saying, "I quit."

Everyone needs direction, and everyone will need training, but if your recruits are not relying on you to motivate them because they are self-motivated, they will succeed more quickly and with less exertion on your part. The goal is to make as much money as possible, and this is infinitely easier when you don't have to spend all of your time pushing your recruits forward. Again, be the example of what you would like to see in your team. In that same vein, here are a couple of key phrases that many networkers use to describe people who you may not want to spend too much time on. One is "don't try to push a wet rope" and the other is "it is infinitely easier to give birth to a new recruit than it is to bring an existing recruit back from the dead."

Never Stop Prospecting

There is no problem that getting a new recruit won't solve. Fresh recruits will help fix the mind-set of the group. Fresh recruits bring youthful optimism to the organization. People reflect the attitudes of those around them. A bright-eyed recruit can turn the organizational mind-set around.

If you have people in your downline who tend to stay bitter—if they are frustrated and refuse to switch up their strategies—chalk them up as a loss. It doesn't feel great, but that is energy that you can put toward training the bold and energetic individuals. Always be on the lookout for strong recruits. Always be searching for all-stars. They can come from unexpected places and tangential connections, which means that you should always be open-minded and optimistic when meeting new people.

Nurture but Don't Baby-sit

Some people will get frustrated. You cannot fix negative people. Of course, everyone has bad days. I am not saying that you should cut people loose when they have a bad day or a bad sales month. I am saying that you have to remove toxic individuals before their negative mind-sets corrupt the entire team. The goal in network marketing is to develop a team of passionate, motivated individuals who can get back up when they fall down. Your job is to provide them with the tools to succeed, but you can't force them to succeed. At a certain point, they will have to take personal responsibility for a lack of production. I like to see how individuals handle stress and frustration, because these are key ingredients to ultimately being successful.

It is often said that distributors in network marketing who work with a rotating list of 300 prospects make at least $100,000 a year, and individuals who work with a rotating list of over 500 prospects make at least $300,000 a year (these numbers are extrapolated from my personal experience as well as from distributors I've recruited). Your prospecting list will be your key to success and prosperity. Grab a legal pad; go to your contact list in your mobile phone and start writing down their names on a piece of paper. Get them out of your phone so that you can focus on them. This is, effectively, your business plan, so you should have it in as many places as possible to remind you who you should be contacting next. Don't just leave this list in your phone.

Prospecting Diagram

Start with a list of 100 names and numbers. Some people may say that they don't have 100 names in their phone. That's fine—this is when you pull out a memory jogger and assist them in writing down names of people from places that they frequent or people from whom they purchase goods and services. Try to expand this list over time to at least 300 names.

You shouldn't just write down the names of everyone you know. You should discriminate. Think of the people who cannot afford the start–up costs—you can approach them later. Think of your unmotivated friends and relatives—you may never even try to recruit them. Your friends and family members comprise your warm prospect list and your initial business plan.

Approaching the right kind of people first can mean a lot to your new distributor's success and confidence. So let's begin our business by trying to recruit the people who we know are always successful in whatever they do—with the assistance of your upline leader, of course—because these will be the people who will most likely intimidate you the most. The great part about trying to recruit the people in this group is that regardless of whether you win or lose, they will respect you even more.

After you have put a warm prospecting list together, you can add a cold prospecting list to it. Cold prospects are individuals with whom you have little to no relationship. This could be a principal at your kid's school, a neighbor who you have little interaction with, etc.

Cold prospects can also be even further removed. You can gain cold prospects while handing out fliers at the mall, through social media, or through prospect lists. This graph from https://www.worldsite.ws/idn/commissions.dhtml gives you an Idea of what your organization could look like if you took this business seriously:

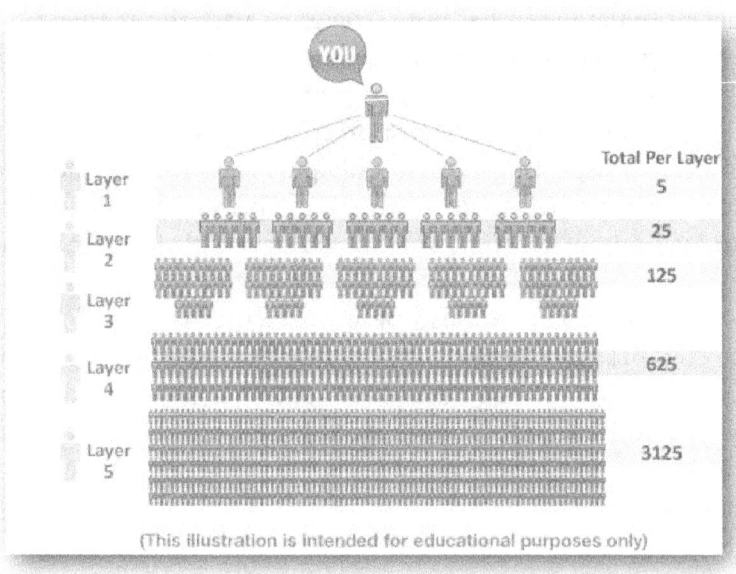

Prospecting in Your Everyday Life

Always have four or five business cards in your hand. Plan on giving them out to as many people as possible each day, but, more importantly, focus on collecting each prospect's contact information so that you can continue to expand your prospecting list. It helps if you store your business cards in your car, rather than at home. They do you no good whatsoever when they are stashed in your home. You can keep extras in your pocket, but keep four or five in your hand. You will never forget to hand them out if they are in your hand.

If your cards are in your pocket or purse, you will frequently forget to pass them out. When you go to pick up your dry cleaning, hand out some cards and talk to the people there about what you do. When you are going out to eat and you overhear people at a nearby table talking about financial frustrations, hand them cards, and get their information in return.

When you are walking your dog and encounter someone you have never seen before, give him or her a business card. You never know which card will be worth it, and there is no harm in trying. I knew of an individual who would start his day at a busy subway station. Every day he would go there and stay until he had passed out at least one hundred business cards and collected as many names and numbers.

The majority of those cards didn't pay off, but he ended up making a lot of money from the few he did connect with. By prospecting everywhere that you go, you will get over any fear that you may have of doing presentations. Put yourself out there. Show the world that you are confident and that you believe in the product and in yourself.

Should You Use Lead–Generating Services?

You can use lead–generation programs and networks if you like, but be sure of their success rate. Try to avoid spending money on any lead generation or marketing services before you have made some major money in the business. Lead–generation programs allow you to purchase leads from an individual or an organization. These leads are typically from people who have opted into various mailing lists for various reasons. They run the gamut from low to high quality. Conversion rates on these leads are usually not that good, one percent or so. However, some people swear by them.

Use Social Media; it's Free!

Social media platforms provide modern distributors with instant access to an infinite field of cold prospects that can be harnessed, but you must know what you are doing. You must know how to approach your audience, and you must realize how much digital noise there is. Some people regard these platforms as magical places that money flows from without a lot of hard work. That is not true. While you can garner a great deal of success, there is still a lot of work involved (but the cost is usually only your time).

I practice some digital strategies, but I keep the majority of my prospecting and recruiting in the realm of face–to–face. Yes, I'm still a little old–fashioned; however, I am trying to become more and more social media savvy to boost my recruiting skills via the Web. I am not trying to talk you out of using social media, just making you aware that it does require time and consistency. If you want to use these technologies, you should first be aware of how many other things you are competing with for these people's attention.

In a face–to–face conversation, you have a captive audience, while in the digital world; you must compete with everything else that is popping up on your prospects' screens from the Internet. Your marketing materials will need to be clear, concise, and interesting enough to hold the prospect's attention. Websites are valuable marketing tools, and so are social media accounts. I mostly use these platforms to provide additional information to my prospects. The platforms are also terrific for staying in contact with prospects and recruits.

Fear of Rejection

A lot of people are intimidated by the idea of prospecting people they don't know. You may think strangers are rejecting you as a person, but that's usually not true. Some people are just so caught up in their day-to-day lives that they can't handle another thing to think about at that time.

That doesn't discredit the opportunity that you are offering them, nor does it discredit you. Let's work to get over this fear. Go to the mall. Go to bars. Go to bookstores. Just talk to people. Be brave and put yourself out there. Yes, some people will reject you, but that doesn't mean that you are not on to something that you will eventually become wealthy in doing.

How to Manage Rejection

I tell my recruits to make rejection a part of their business plan. Statistically, 80 percent of those you prospect will say no to your opportunity, and on average about 20 percent of the people you prospect will say yes. The 80/20 rule (also called the Pareto Principle or the Law of the Vital Few) is a very valuable tool for you to understand, especially if you have never worked in a sales capacity throughout your career. It also translates into what you can expect from your team members, which is that on average about 80 percent of your team's production will come from just 20 percent of the people on your team.

That means that 80 percent of your personal recruits will come from 20 percent of the people that you personally contact and do a presentation for. Typically this also means that approximately 80 percent of your commission and income will come from the most focused 20 percent of your working team members. Over time, you will figure out approximately how many people may give you a no before you get a yes. Look at it as though you are getting your rejections out of the way.

The 80/20 Rule Drilled Down

One in five prospects will want to hear about your opportunity (20 percent).

One in five of those people will be interested in your opportunity (20 percent).

One in five of those people will have the drive necessary to take advantage of your opportunity (20 percent).

One in five of those people will build a successful business (20 percent).

It only takes five to ten frontline superstars, depending on the compensation plan, to make you a whole lot of money in most network marketing companies. That means you just have to use the 80/20 rule to figure out how many presentations you have to do personally. And then you have to use it to figure out how many people you have to personally recruit to get five to ten frontline superstars who will have the drive, the skill, the viable network of family and friends, and the willingness to convert strangers into recruits who will each build their own frontline of five to ten frontline superstars.

If you want five to ten successful frontline people who will make a lot of money in their businesses—thus making you a whole lot of money in up-front bonuses and overrides—you will need to personally recruit twenty-five to fifty frontline distributors (20 percent of 25 = 5 or 20 percent of 50 = 10). This is only for those people who are trying to get to at least a six-figure or more annual income in the business. Now, some networkers may try to argue this point and say that my numbers are a bit high. Well, truthfully they may be a bit low. If you know a networker who is making a lot of money with a company, say $10,000 to $20,000 monthly or more, ask this person to show you his or her back office and break down how many people are actively producing today, and how many of the people that he or she personally recruited quit and had to be replaced. Ask this networker to show you his or her figures. As you can see, I have no problem showing you mine.

Now, to personally recruit twenty-five frontline people, on average you will need to do approximately 125 presentations to prospects (friends, family, and strangers) (20 percent of 125 = 25). On average 20 percent of them will really be serious enough (20 percent of 25 = 5) to actually want to build a successful business. This is how you get your five serious frontline recruits.

The same logic applies if you are aiming to get ten personal frontline recruits who will be big business builders—you need to personally do 250 presentations to prospects (family, friends, and strangers) to get fifty people who will sign up as distributors. Ten of those fifty will be serious business builders (20 percent of 250 = 50 and 20 percent of 50 = 10). Now, the great part about technology is that these presentations can be done in a variety of forums from face- to-face to Skype to having someone watch a YouTube video to handing him or her a DVD of the presentation. Use all the tools that are available to you to get your message out. Once you have done your part—your personal recruiting—the magic of making money can really begin. Now you have team members who can duplicate what you have done.

Now you have the opportunity to capitalize on what we in the network marketing industry call the eighth and ninth wonders of the world. The first of these wonders is the magic of compound recruiting (when your recruits are bringing in scores of new recruits without any effort from you personally, and you are getting paid handsomely on them, as your upline did on you). And the second wonder is asset leveraging (I would rather earn 1% from 100 people's efforts than 100% from my own efforts – John D. Rockefeller).

For some, especially the first timers, these can be daunting figures, but over time, they will become less daunting. Look at it like this: if you want five people to join, you only need to present to 25 people. If you want to personally present to 25 people, you will need to contact 125 people on average about setting up a place and time to do so. So, if you contact 125 people you will end up with about 5 new recruits and one talented recruit who will put in the hard work to build a major business. Over time, your reach will expand because as your team grows, your distributors will be duplicating your efforts, and eventually people will have heard so much about what is going on that they may start calling you to ask you to present to them so that they can find out first–hand what all the excitement is about.

The Goal of Prospecting

Whenever you talk to people, be they warm prospects or cold prospects, your end goal should be to get your presentations in front of them. The best networkers understand that the real money is in the follow–up. Many people fail in most sales organizations because they never develop the discipline to get good at the art of the follow–up.

Think of your initial contact as starting the relationship and subsequent follow–ups as necessary contacts to keep the relationship growing. This is how the real builders make their money. It may take several attempts to get your prospect's attention, but when you do, make sure that you have a system in place for following up with him or her periodically, as your ultimate goal is to get your prospect to view a company presentation.

Again, this presentation can be a home meeting, a hotel meeting, a video or DVD, or even a phone presentation. It is also fine to prospect with scripts. Many large teams are built quickly because new and seasoned distributors on that team use the same scripts to prospect and invite people to watch via video or attend a live presentation.

A script just helps you to demonstrate to you and your team the basic information that you will need to quickly convey to prospects to get them in front of a presentation. Below are two examples of scripts that you can use and tweak to get prospects out to a presentation, whether they are family members, coworkers, or people you have recently met.

Here is a sample invitation for a family member, friend, or even someone you have recently met:

You: Hello Mike.... This is Maria. How are you? Prospect: Great. How is the family?

You: Great. (Talk for about two minutes.)

You: Hey Mike, I'm calling you because I am hosting a grand opening party to share information about my new business. Since I have really learned to value your opinion, I would like to get your feedback about what I am doing. My new business partners will be in town this week to share information about the business opportunity with a few very select people that I am inviting to my home. Can I count on you to attend and celebrate with me and get the information for yourself at (location/date/time)? By the way, I'm pretty sure it's something that you're going to like!

Prospect: Okay, but can you tell me what this is all about?

You: Well, since I'm new, I would rather have you get the information from my new business partners, who are experts at explaining the business opportunity.

Prospect: Okay, I believe I can make it, I will see you there.

And here is an over the phone invitation for someone you have recently met:

P (Prospect): Hello...

Y (You): Hello, (P). This is (Your Name). How are you?

P: Great. How are you?

Y: Great. (Talk for about two minutes).

Y: I'm having a private party for some close friends to show some exclusive products you won't find anywhere else. Can you join us at (location/date/time)?

P: OK, great! I'll see you then.

Every month you must plan for the following:

1. how many people you can contact
2. how many people you and your upline can present to
3. how many people you can get to join
4. how many people you can get to build

Additionally, who are other good candidates for network marketing?

- teens over eighteen
- college students
- recent college graduates
- recent college graduates with student loan debt
- people younger than thirty who want more job satisfaction, money, children, and a better life.

CHAPTER 9

How to Build a Team

Build from Event to Event?

From the local Tuesday night meeting, to the regional rally, to the leadership summit, to the national meetings, these are the events that you must get as many of your team members as possible to regularly participate in. It's always clear who the big income earners are going to be with every company. It's always the people who understand implicitly that their teams must be full participants in all company events.

Many of your team members won't come to the business with the understanding that it's not just about them attending the meetings for you because you asked them to attend, but that it's about them understanding that their team is going to mimic what they do and don't do. Therefore, you will have to train and drill this over and over if you want to get to the pot of gold at the end of the rainbow in network marketing. If the events are made fun and motivational, and you can get a few of your team members to attend the first few, their excitement when they return will help you convince the others to attend future events with little difficulty.

The majority of distributors in network marketing work their businesses on a part–time basis. And yet you will hear about people who are making the big money in network marketing because they have built huge national and international teams, and these people are fortunate enough to be able to do the business full time. Better still, their incomes are even higher when they have people on their teams who are consistently making enough money from their efforts and the efforts of their teams that they can do the business full time as well. How does this happen?

The average full–time network marketer and recruiter usually gets there because he or she develops a habit, a schedule, and a routine of doing at least four home business opportunity presentations (BOPs) per week in his or her home, a team member's home, or even at a prospect's home. That means an average of about sixteen in–home BOPs per month, over an extended period.

I urge you, because I know you have it within you, to set as your goal with the company that you decide to join that at some point along the way you would like to build a large enough team that you have the ability to make the choice to become a full–time distributor. If you want an income that can weather any storm, make it your goal to help as many of your team members as possible to become full–time leaders as well. Imagine being full time in your business and also being fortunate enough to have twenty–one full–time recruiters on your team doing an average of four BOPs per week. That would be an average of 336 presentations per month being conducted in your organization.

This is what wealth looks like in the network marketing industry: your income is rock solid not just when you can afford to do the business full time, but when five to ten of your frontline recruits are earning enough money to go full time in the business as well. Let's be clear; your income will not be solid in this business until several of your frontline recruits are also reaching their income goals in your company. This wonderful full–time network marketer lifestyle can continue for decades, as long as your company stays in business and doesn't make many bad decisions that, in turn, drive your leaders away from the company.

If You Want Your Team to Recruit, You Must Do It First

If you want to be a mentor, to train your new recruits, you must intrinsically understand the business. You must learn to understand the business, and you must learn to become a very good recruiter yourself. You can't expect your team members to listen to you if they don't see the fruits of your labor as a recruiter.

They will want to see your recruiting stats, which will make them believers in what you are espousing, and, if they follow in your footsteps, that could translate into big checks for them and for you. This is important because your prospects will want to see your paychecks as well if they are savvy and have read this book. They won't necessarily ask for proof because they don't trust you; rather, they will want to be able to set realistic income expectations.

Organize Your Calendar

Some of the most effective individuals in network marketing still use paper calendars for planning. Paper calendars allow a better visualization of the next thirty to sixty days. Digital calendars are fine for tracking activities as well, but often they take more time to sift or scroll through. With a paper calendar, you can simply glance at it and see your next month, next two months, or next three months of planned activity.

Success or failure in network marketing is directly related to how successfully you interact with your calendar. Track your personal schedule and your presentation schedule. Track the presentation schedules of your team. You should always know when the next presentation is scheduled for you and for your leaders as well.

A part–time distributor needs to make at least three one–on–one or group presentations a week. Here is an example of a part–time distributor's schedule:

Monday, Wednesday, and Friday
Recruiting presentation with a coworker over lunch or dinner (20–30 minutes).

Tuesday and Thursday
BOP (business opportunity presentation) at someone's home (45 minutes to an hour).

Saturday
Company training (one hour) and a presentation (45 minutes to an hour).

Sunday
BOP at someone's house (one hour).

A full-time distributor's schedule should look like this:

Monday to Thursday, every week:
7:30–8:00 a.m.: motivational call
10:00–11:00 a.m.: face–to–face presentation
2:00–3:00 p.m.: national recruiting call
7:00–9:00 p.m.: BOP

When Recruiting, Focus on the Why

Early in the presentation or conversation, get your prospects to communicate their Why. Figure out what their motivation really is. Ask people, "Why do you want to earn additional income?" Focus them on their Why during the presentation so they don't get sidetracked by the How. Talk about your Why and what you did to achieve it. Discuss the goals that you have set and the goals that you have met.

Set Reasonable Expectations of Success

You shouldn't ever mislead prospects with falsified financial statements. If they ever learn that you have lied to them, they will be bitter and angry with you. Talk about the averages that you have seen. You can talk about the high end of income, but be sure to mention the low end as well. Always remember that in network marketing your reputation is your currency.

Reasons to Cut Recruits Loose

1. They lack a financially viable network.
2. If they have a negative sphere of influence, e.g., people run away from them rather than toward them when it comes to business conversations, you may have to turn them loose.

What Is the Difference Between Joining and Building?

As a serious business builder, you will work hard to build your business and your network. A conservative number that you could target to be considered a serious business builder by your upline, within thirty–six months of starting your team building, could be between $5,000 and $6,000 a month as a part–time distributor. If you have five serious business builders who are making $5,000–$6,000 a month on a part–time basis, then you should be (depending on your compensation plan) making at least $10,000 a month without lifting a finger.

People who just join to be part of the excitement may not be motivated enough to build a big team. I imagine that you are wondering why you would recruit that kind of person in the first place if he or she is not that motivated. Unfortunately, there is no way of predetermining who is or who is not motivated to build a big team until after you have all begun working together. A recruit might be very hard working in the corporate world, but he or she may lack the qualities that make a strong self–starter as an entrepreneur. Remember that every phone call, every business card, every presentation, and yes, even every rejection, draws you closer to those five to ten frontline superstars that you will need to build a successful network marketing team. In turn, this team will get you closer to achieving your financial goal for your business, whether it is $10,000, $20,000, or $30,000 a month or more that you are seeking.

CHAPTER 10

Coaching and Mentoring

Network marketing is an adult version of follow–the–leader, except that you can make money, and in some cases, a whole lot of money, playing this game. In network marketing, being or learning how to become a good recruiter is going to have a great impact in determining how your team views your leadership skills. You will need to know or learn how to train your recruits in the fine art of prospecting and recruiting if you want to get them up and running as quickly as possible.

Be open and honest with your recruits. Be approachable, but still set limitations. If you still have a job and you can't be available at times, tell your recruits. Let them know what the boundaries are and stick to those boundaries. Don't allow them to contact you whenever they feel like it, as this will lead to calls at three in the morning.

If you don't remember anything else that I have shared in this book when you start out with your new or next network marketing company, please remember this: the speed of the leader is the speed of the pack. Set the pace for your team. Set the expectations that you have for your team. Set expected sales and recruiting targets and schedules with your team.

You can always incentivize them with small but meaningful rewards. Lunch, a small bonus, or something of that nature always spawns friendly competition. Keep team members motivated and moving forward. Don't trust that their desire to make money will be all the incentive that they will need—everyone needs a little push from time to time.

Set a Strong Example

You must consistently produce as a leader so that you can set a strong example for your team to follow. No one will listen to you if you are pushing your team members to produce but they don't see regular production from you. You won't keep their respect if you aren't leading the way. Here is a good piece of advice that a mentor once gave me: don't ever ask someone to do something that you can't do or won't do. Be a strong leader and a team player. If your team members see you as a strong leader, then your praise and compliments will be more meaningful to them.

Show Them

You have to be able to look at a recruit and say, "This is what I did to get here. Let me lead you to that place." Show your recruits that you know what you are doing and that you know how to get them there. Show them that your advice is sound and actionable. Show them that you care and want them to succeed. If your recruits know that you want them to succeed, they will work even harder to succeed.

Give Your Time to the Recruits Who Deserve It

Figure out who wants your mentoring. Then figure out who deserves it. I don't work with distributors who want my time; I work with distributors who deserve my time. If they are giving 100 percent, I am with them all the way.

But if they make constant excuses as to why they can't participate in training and other events that will lead to their success, I am less likely to isolate valuable time to work with that person directly. Give your energy and attention to deserving people and producers. Constantly talk to your team members about their individual goals, and then do everything in your power to help them reach those goals. They will be forever grateful.

Again, Remember the Why

Again, talk to your team members about their Why. Share yours. Keep their Why in front of them when they start to get discouraged. Give them the tools to motivate themselves, but still provide support. Your goal is to build a strong and mutually beneficial relationship. Constantly review their production goals with them. They will learn from you how to stay focused on their production goals.

Remember Your Mentor

Remember what your mentor did right and what your mentor did wrong. Remember the questions that constantly ran through your mind. Try to be a better mentor to your team members than your mentor was to you, even if your mentor was great. Tie your success to your team members' successes. Help them to identify the areas that they are having trouble with, and help them to move through these challenges.

You Don't Need Luck

So now you have the tools. Now you have enough information to find the right company and mentor that fits your goals and your personality. You were born with the will to succeed. This is where I send you out into the world to make your fortune. Welcome to making it big in network marketing. I have very high expectations for you, and I am confident that you will exceed those as well. Most people would say, "Good luck!" I am not one of those people. The quote that I will leave you with, which I am particularly fond of, is from Louis Pasteur (who invented antibiotics and the pasteurization process). He said, "Always remember, fortune favors the prepared mind."

If you are a leader or looking to become a leader in a network marketing/direct sales business and you want me and my team to assist you and your team members in reaching that $5,000–$10,000's in income mark or more, part-time and retiring earlier, please see www.moatscoaching.com. We coach many distributors from many different companies and we don't affiliate with any company so there will never be a conflict or concern of cross-recruiting.

Exhibit 1

EXCEL TELECOMMUNICATIONS, INC.

CHECK NO.

MONTHLY LDU COMMISSION

PAY PERIOD: 09/01/95 TO 09/30/95

MOATS, DAMON

Level	No Cust	LDU	Commission	Your Organization Level	MR	SLS	AC
0	49	772.40	21.23	1	29		10
1	306	3,174.00	14.64	2	68		14
2	473	5,441.50	13.60	3	57	1	8
3	346	3,052.56	7.64	4	37		9
4	225	3,133.49	7.82	5	26		6
5	171	1,725.00	4.32	6	26		1
6	159	807.22	5.60	7	14		5
7	173	2,034.35	90.20				

TOTAL COMMISSION 165.05

PRIOR ACCUM BALANCE

PAGES OVER 20 CHG

CHECK CHARGE 3.00

NET CHECK AMOUNT 162.05

	YEAR TO DATE SUMMARY
Jan	0.00
Feb	0.00
Mar	0.00
Apr	0.00
May	0.00
Jun	1,201.00
Jul	2,436.00
Aug	3,446.35
Sep	3,934.75
Oct	3,774.45
Nov	269.05

TOT	15,061.60

```
*************************
* Year To Date Summary *
*     Includes         *
*Weekly&Monthly Checks *
*************************
```

113

Exhibit 2

4424904

```
                    MONTHLY LDU COMMISSION                        YEAR TO DATE
PAY PERIOD:  05/01/96 TO 05/31/96                                    SUMMARY
MOATS, DAMON
                                   Your Organization       Jan      4,694.82
Level  No Cust      LDU   Commission  Level  MR  SLS  AC    Feb      4,293.17
  0        72    926.17       35.52     1    39       18 Mar      7,211.69
  1       491  5,226.93       26.88     2   130       33 Apr      9,182.62
  2       945 14,525.66       36.31     3   114       21 May      9,172.77
  3       833 10,455.37       26.15     4   117   2   27 Jun      5,048.90
  4       919 11,460.47       28.70     5   145       23 Jul        521.33
  5     1,032 11,233.41       28.08     6   126       14     -----------
  6       970  9,484.73       63.12     7    74   1   12 TOT     40,125.30
  7       632  6,131.50      242.17

TOTAL COMMISSION            486.93        ***************************
PRIOR ACCUM BALANCE                       * Year To Date Summary *
PAGES OVER 20 CHG             .60         *      Includes        *
CHECK CHARGE                              *Weekly&Monthly Checks *
NET CHECK AMOUNT           486.33         ***************************
```

Exhibit 3

4800289

```
                    MONTHLY LDU COMMISSION
PAY PERIOD:   07/01/96 TO 07/31/96
MOATS, DAMON
```

Level	No Cust	LDU	Commission
0	72	1,844.08	57.64
1	520	6,458.70	33.10
2	978	12,401.48	30.99
3	901	12,327.40	30.80
4	950	10,775.38	26.96
5	1,162	10,635.01	26.58
6	1,144	10,011.17	65.43
7	713	7,884.27	302.24

Your Organization

Level	MR	SLS	AC
1	39		18
2	132		33
3	125	2	22
4	122		27
5	162		27
6	146		15
7	85	1	13

YEAR TO DATE SUMMARY

Jan	4,694.82
Feb	4,293.17
Mar	7,211.69
Apr	9,182.62
May	9,172.77
Jun	5,048.90
Jul	4,402.33
Aug	4,952.18
Sep	967.74
TOT	49,926.22

```
TOTAL COMMISSION         573.74
PRIOR ACCUM BALANCE
PAGES OVER 20 CHG          1.00
CHECK CHARGE
NET CHECK AMOUNT         572.74

************************************
* Year To Date Summary *
*       Includes        *
*Weekly&Monthly Checks  *
************************************
```

Exhibit 4

Damon Moats
Fulltime
Former occupation: Medical Sales
Best month: $54,385

Exhibit 5

Exhibit 6

Exhibit 7

Maxx it Up '99

Exhibit 8

Exhibit 9

MOATS, DAMON (ED)
Period of 09/01/96 - 09/30/96
(LDU: 75 Cust, 33 ACIV, 43 NS)

Amount	Rate	Comm	0 1 2 3 4 5 6 7 / Acctno Status Svc Date Lst Call Trm Date	AR	Senior	RegDir	ExecDir	SD
41.63	0.25%	0.10	ANTHONY M RICE (05/03/95),AR,AC (Cust= 33 ACTV= 6)	(HESTER)	(FIELDS)	(FIELDS)	(ORBERSON)	(None)
223.54	0.25%	0.56	CHARDOT LTD (05/17/95),OMR (Cust= 27 ACTV= 14)	(HESTER)	(FIELDS)	(FIELDS)	(ORBERSON)	(None)
1.49	1.00%	0.01	DELIVERANCE INT'L INC (06/22/95)(C),MR (Cust= 8 ACTV= 3)	(HESTER)	(FIELDS)	(FIELDS)	(ORBERSON)	(None)
0.00	0.25%	0.00	DELIVERANCE INT'L INC (06/22/95)(C),MR (Cust= 1 ACTV= 0)	(HESTER)	(FIELDS)	(FIELDS)	(ORBERSON)	(None)
0.00	1.00%	0.00	JACQUELINE M SHORT (06/22/95)(C),MR (Cust= 1 ACTV= 0)	(HESTER)	(FIELDS)	(FIELDS)	(ORBERSON)	(None)
0.00	0.25%	0.00	JACQUELINE M SHORT (08/02/95)(C),MR (Cust= 1 ACTV= 0)	(HESTER)	(FIELDS)	(FIELDS)	(ORBERSON)	(None)
0.00	1.00%	0.00	JEFFREY HAYNES (08/02/95)(C),MR (Cust= 3 ACTV= 0)	(HESTER)	(FIELDS)	(FIELDS)	(ORBERSON)	(None)
0.00	0.25%	0.00	JEFFREY HAYNES (08/02/95)(C),MR (Cust= 1 ACTV= 0)	(HESTER)	(FIELDS)	(FIELDS)	(ORBERSON)	(None)
10.07	1.00%	0.10	CURTIS J ANDERSON (09/19/95)(C),MR (Cust= 4 ACTV= 2)	(HESTER)	(FIELDS)	(FIELDS)	(ORBERSON)	(None)
0.00	1.00%	0.00	DIANE GREENIDGE (09/19/95)(C),MR (Cust= 1 ACTV= 0)	(HESTER)	(FIELDS)	(FIELDS)	(ORBERSON)	(None)
0.00	0.25%	0.00	DIANE GREENIDGE (09/19/95)(C),MR (Cust= 1 ACTV= 0)	(HESTER)	(FIELDS)	(FIELDS)	(ORBERSON)	(None)
12.70	5.00%	0.64	ANTHONY M GREENIDGE (01/02/96),MR (Cust= 8 ACTV= 4)	(HESTER)	(FIELDS)	(FIELDS)	(ORBERSON)	(None)
30.86	1.00%	0.31	RITA Y EVERETTE (09/19/95)(C),MR (Cust= 4 ACTV= 1)	(HESTER)	(FIELDS)	(FIELDS)	(ORBERSON)	(None)
5.74	1.00%	0.06	GWENDOLYN E JONES (10/13/95),MR (Cust= 2 ACTV= 1)	(HESTER)	(FIELDS)	(FIELDS)	(ORBERSON)	(None)
0.00	0.25%	0.00	GWENDOLYN E JONES (10/13/95),MR (Cust= 1 ACTV= 0)	(HESTER)	(FIELDS)	(FIELDS)	(ORBERSON)	(None)
105.06	5.00%	5.25	JAMAL PARKER (06/25/96),MR (Cust= 4 ACTV= 1)	(HESTER)	(FIELDS)	(FIELDS)	(ORBERSON)	(None)
122.09	1.00%	1.22	SYLVESTER SOLOMON (11/13/95),MR (Cust= 13 ACTV= 6)	(HESTER)	(FIELDS)	(FIELDS)	(ORBERSON)	(None)
98.31	1.00%	0.98	CIEJAN INC (11/17/95),MR (Cust= 31 ACTV= 12)	(HESTER)	(FIELDS)	(FIELDS)	(ORBERSON)	(None)
1.39	0.25%	0.00	KEITH A GREENE (04/16/96),MR (Cust= 4 ACTV= 0)	(HESTER)	(FIELDS)	(FIELDS)	(ORBERSON)	(None)
82.09	0.25%	0.21	PAUL B WINGATE (05/22/95),RD,QAC (Cust= 25 ACTV= 12)	(BUSSEY)	(FIELDS)	(FIELDS)	(ORBERSON)	(None)
23.83	0.25%	0.06	REALTY HOLDINGS LTD (05/22/95),OMR,AC (Cust= 22 ACTV= 8)	(BUSSEY)	(FIELDS)	(FIELDS)	(ORBERSON)	(None)
189.72	1.00%	1.90	FREDDIE L FLAKES (05/22/95),OMR,AC (Cust= 33 ACTV= 17)	(BUSSEY)	(FIELDS)	(FIELDS)	(ORBERSON)	(None)
87.84	0.25%	0.22	FREDDIE L FLAKES (05/22/95),OMR,AC (Cust= 4 ACTV= 3)	(BUSSEY)	(FIELDS)	(FIELDS)	(ORBERSON)	(None)
172.64	5.00%	8.63	JANELL C SUTTON (06/14/96),MR (Cust= 4 ACTV= 1)	(BUSSEY)	(FIELDS)	(FIELDS)	(ORBERSON)	(None)
0.00	5.00%	0.00	JANELL C SUTTON (06/14/96),MR (Cust= 2 ACTV= 0)	(BUSSEY)	(FIELDS)	(FIELDS)	(ORBERSON)	(None)
93.88	2.00%	1.88	DORREN M LEWIS (06/15/96),MR (Cust= 2 ACTV= 1)	(BUSSEY)	(FIELDS)	(FIELDS)	(ORBERSON)	(None)
0.00	1.00%	0.00	DORREN M LEWIS (06/15/96),MR (Cust= 3 ACTV= 3)	(BUSSEY)	(FIELDS)	(FIELDS)	(ORBERSON)	(None)
0.00	0.25%	0.00	JIMMIE J GREEN (11/07/96),MR (Cust= 0 ACTV= 0)	(PENDING)	(FIELDS)	(FIELDS)	(ORBERSON)	(None)
73.55	5.00%	3.68	MICHEAL BOZEMAN (05/22/95)(C),MR (Cust= 11 ACTV= 2)	(BUSSEY)	(FIELDS)	(FIELDS)	(ORBERSON)	(None)
49.01	2.00%	0.98	MICHEAL BOZEMAN (05/22/95)(C),MR (Cust= 1 ACTV= 0)	(BUSSEY)	(FIELDS)	(FIELDS)	(ORBERSON)	(None)
0.00	1.00%	0.00	PAMELA B MOORE (05/22/95)(C),MR (Cust= 23 ACTV= 6)	(BUSSEY)	(FIELDS)	(FIELDS)	(ORBERSON)	(None)
0.00	0.25%	0.00	PAMELA B MOORE (05/22/95)(C),MR (Cust= 2 ACTV= 2)	(BUSSEY)	(FIELDS)	(FIELDS)	(ORBERSON)	(None)
8.25	1.00%	0.08	DERRICK CARTER (05/22/95)(C),MR (Cust= 1 ACTV= 0)	(REALTY HO)	(FIELDS)	(FIELDS)	(ORBERSON)	(None)
0.00	0.25%	0.00	DERRICK CARTER (05/22/95)(C),MR (Cust= 1 ACTV= 1)	(REALTY HO)	(FIELDS)	(FIELDS)	(ORBERSON)	(None)
253.48	1.00%	2.53	MONTROSE MATTHEWS (05/22/95)(C),MR (Cust= 3 ACTV= 3)	(REALTY HO)	(FIELDS)	(FIELDS)	(ORBERSON)	(None)
150.11	0.25%	0.38	AARON C WRIGHT (05/22/95),RD,OAC (Cust= 15 ACTV= 9)	(REALTY HO)	(FIELDS)	(FIELDS)	(ORBERSON)	(None)
267.36	5.00%	13.37	AARON C WRIGHT (05/22/95),RD,OAC (Cust= 15 ACTV= 10)	(REALTY HO)	(FIELDS)	(FIELDS)	(ORBERSON)	(None)
14.36	2.00%	0.29	VINCENTE S MOORE (05/12/95)(C),OMR,AC (Cust= 25 ACTV= 8)	(REALTY HO)	(FIELDS)	(FIELDS)	(ORBERSON)	(None)
			VINCENTE S MOORE (05/12/95)(C),OMR,AC (Cust= 2 ACTV= 2)	(REALTY HO)	(FIELDS)	(FIELDS)	(ORBERSON)	(None)

Exhibit 10

EXCEL TELECOMMUNICATIONS

TM002200 Page 33

MOATS, DAMON (ED)

Period of 01/01/97 - 01/31/97

Amount	Rate	Comm	(LD 0 1 2 3 4 5 6 7	84/ 38 PG	Acctno Status	Svc Date Lst Call Trm Date	AR	Senior	RegDir	ExecDir	SD
43.85	1.00%	0.44	- JOHN GRAYSON (09/24/96),MR(LD= 2/ 0)		/)		(MOATS	)(MOATS	)(MOATS	)(MOATS	)(None)
0.00	0.25%	0.00	- JEFFREY CANADY (09/24/96),MR(LD= 0/ 0)				(MOATS	)(MOATS	)(MOATS	)(MOATS	)(None)
8.20	1.00%	0.08	- JEFFREY CANADY (09/24/96),MR(LD= 8/ 2)				(MOATS	)(MOATS	)(MOATS	)(MOATS	)(None)
49.06	0.25%	0.12	- PHOEBE C ALLEN (09/24/96)(C),MR(LD= 3/ 3)				(MOATS	)(MOATS	)(MOATS	)(MOATS	)(None)
35.35	0.25%	0.09	- TERI L HUDSON (09/30/96),MR(LD= 3/ 3)				(MOATS	)(MOATS	)(MOATS	)(MOATS	)(None)
27.90	1.00%	0.28	- TERI L HUDSON (09/30/96),MR(LD= 5/ 4)				(MOATS	)(MOATS	)(MOATS	)(MOATS	)(None)
0.00	0.25%	0.00	- MERCEDES M FRAZIER (09/30/96),MR(LD= 1/ 0)				(MOATS	)(MOATS	)(MOATS	)(MOATS	)(None)
0.00	1.00%	0.00	- MERCEDES M FRAZIER (09/30/96),MR(LD= 3/ 0)				(MOATS	)(MOATS	)(MOATS	)(MOATS	)(None)

495.42	LDU Commissions Earned
-2.00	Pages Over 20 Charge
.00	Paging Commissions Earned
493.42	Net Check Amount

```
**************************************************************
**                                                          **
** All SMB customers with a service date prior to June 1, 1996 had  **
** a commercial account worth 2 points and received commercial LDU  **
** commission. As of June 1, 1996 the SMB accounts will represent   **
** the new "Simply One" product and will be a residential account   **
** worth 1 point with residential LDU commission.           **
**                                                          **
**************************************************************
```

Exhibit 11

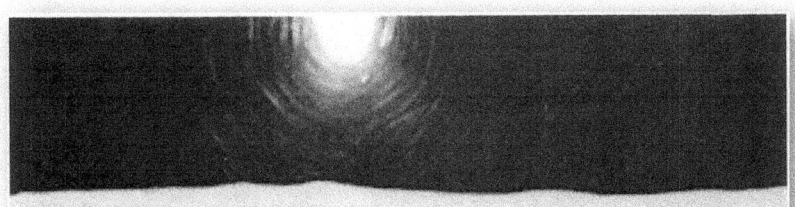

Maxxis 2000, Inc.
1901 Montreal Road
Tucker, GA 30084.

Indented Binary Genealo

CC # : 2414D

_C_	_Ctr_	Name
7D	001	Frank, Jean Claude
7D	003	Frank, Jean Claude
'D	002	Frank, Jean Claude

Exhibit 12

on D.

Page   1

Date   April 2, 2002

Time   12:57:43PM

Rank	Sponsor Name	Sponsor CC	.Ctr
PD	R.J.S. Holdings	1038D	2
PD	Moats,Damon D.	2414D	1
ED	Moats,Damon D.	2414D	3
ED	D D M Group	2419D	1
ASC	D D M Group	2419D	3
ASC	Watts, Wanda	13425D	1
ASC	Watts, Wanda	13425D	1
		2280D	2

Exhibit 13

	Ctr	Name	Period	Lvl
D	001	Moats,Damon D.	1	0
D	003	Moats,Damon D.	1	1
D	001	D D M Group	1	2
D	003	D D M Group	1	3
5D	001	Watts, Wanda	16	4
5D	003	Watts, Wanda	16	5
5D	002	Watts, Wanda	16	
D	001	Forbes,Reginald L.	161	
D	003	Forbes,Reginald L.	161	
D	001	Jenkins,Shawn Q.	161	
D	003	Jenkins,Shawn Q.	161	
D	002	Jenkins,Shawn Q.	161	
D	002	Forbes,Reginald L.	161	
D	001	Thomas,Danny M.	164	
D	003	Thomas,Danny M.	164	
D	002	Thomas,Danny M.	164	
D	001	Powcom Enterprise	1	

Exhibit 14

Period: [Monthly – December 2014]

Level/On,PSC Customer ID Type		Name	Rank	City	POP	POPA
0	77821617	D Damon Moats	Advisor	Fort Washington	00.00	00.00
1	77828828	D Pamela Moats-Davis	Advisor	Cincinnati	00.00	00.00
2	77841780	D maria moats	Advisor	Cincinnati	00.00	00.00
2	77868405	D Joaquin Wilson	Advisor	Cincinnati	00.00	00.00
3	77871725	D Margarethe Roberson	Advisor	Cincinnati	00.00	00.00
5	77984227	C Q Q	Advisor	CINCINNATI	00.00	00.00
4	77974897	C d a	Advisor	cincinnati	00.00	00.00
3	77954046	D TRACI MCKINNEY	Advisor	Cincinnati	00.00	00.00
5	78623830	C x x	Advisor	fayetteville	00.00	00.00
5	78638593	C WENDY MATHIS	Advisor	FAYETTEVILLE	00.00	00.00
3	77954024	D MARK IVERY	Advisor	Cincinnati	00.00	00.00
5	78631338	D DARLENE ROBERTSONDAUGHTER	Advisor	Fayetteville	00.00	00.00
3	77953986	D DONNYELLE SMITH	Advisor	Cincinnati	00.00	00.00
4	77972386	D KIMBERLY C. MIREE	Advisor	Fayetteville	00.00	00.00
2	77888430	D KELLI GOODWIN	Advisor	Cincinnati	00.00	00.00
1	77828838	D ABIGAIL MOATS	Advisor	WILLINGBORO	00.00	00.00
1	77832568	D DIANE MOORE-EUBANKS	Advisor	Burtonsville	00.00	00.00
2	77831769	D Charles Parker	Advisor	Washington	00.00	00.00
4	77984365	C khatol Zaher	Advisor	Alexandria	00.00	00.00
3	77983407	D hawa nawaz	Advisor	Alexandria	00.00	00.00
3	77901972	D monique williams	Advisor	uppermarlboro	00.00	00.00
4	78116192	D Pamela Hardy	Advisor	Temple Hills	00.00	00.00
6	78141622	D Dianeda Short	Advisor	Suitland	00.00	00.00
5	78147665	D Bernedette Shipman	Advisor	Woodbridge	00.00	00.00
5	78194331	D Cathy Reed	Advisor	Oxford	00.00	00.00
5	78116565	C Shirlinette Tyree	Advisor	Glen Dale	00.00	00.00
4	78086707	D Kimberly Contee	Advisor	Hyattsville	00.00	00.00
5	78125045	D Margaret Greer	Advisor	Fort Washington	00.00	00.00
4	78084061	D Janice Wright	Advisor	Lanham	00.00	00.00
5	78219611	D Hardee Green	Advisor	Woodbridge	00.00	00.00
4	78094984	D KENNETH POWELL	Advisor	Fort Washington	00.00	00.00
5	78116627	C shirlinette tyree	Advisor	Glendale	00.00	00.00
6	78139861	D Leron Greer	Advisor	Fort Washington	00.00	00.00
5	78116591	C Shirlinette Tyree	Advisor	Glendale	00.00	00.00
4	78101960	D Sylvia Hughes	Advisor	Lanham	00.00	00.00

Exhibit 15

4	 78169062	D Lavern Mathis-Burwell	Advisor Lanham	00.00 00.00
5	78110498	D shari seegobin	Advisor Jessup	00.00 00.00
5	78116564	C Shirlinette Tyree	Advisor Glen Dale	00.00 00.00
5	78116569	C Shirlinette Tyree	Advisor Glen Dale	00.00 00.00
5	78172225	D Bernice Eason Parker	Advisor Alexandria	00.00 00.00
5	78116566	C Shirlinette Tyree	Advisor Glen Dale	00.00 00.00
4	78086725	D Crystal Scott	Advisor Waldorf	00.00 00.00
5	78122208	D Paula Stevens	Advisor Suitland	00.00 00.00
4	78101946	D Patricia Green	Advisor Woodbridge	00.00 00.00
4	78102014	D Angela Reynolds	Advisor Washington	00.00 00.00
5	78125637	D Joseph A Powell, Jr	Advisor Glenn Dale	00.00 00.00
4	78150782	D Sharnell Jones	Advisor Fort Washington	00.00 00.00
5	78169663	D Naomi Green	Advisor Roxboro	00.00 00.00
4	78150829	D Shirley Williams	Advisor Fort Washington	00.00 00.00
5	78137155	D Eva Randolph	Advisor Woodbridge	00.00 00.00

Page # 1 of 287

Search [SELECT OPTION...] [SELECT OPTION...] Find

Exhibit 16

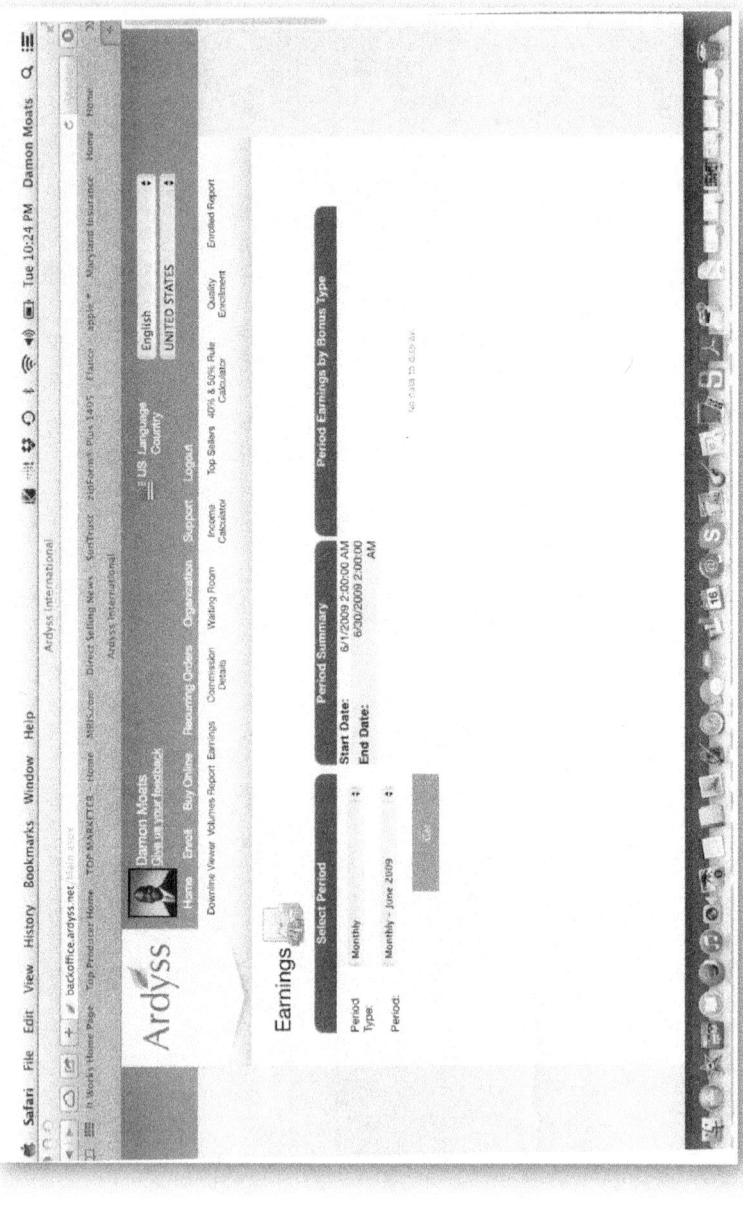

Exhibit 17

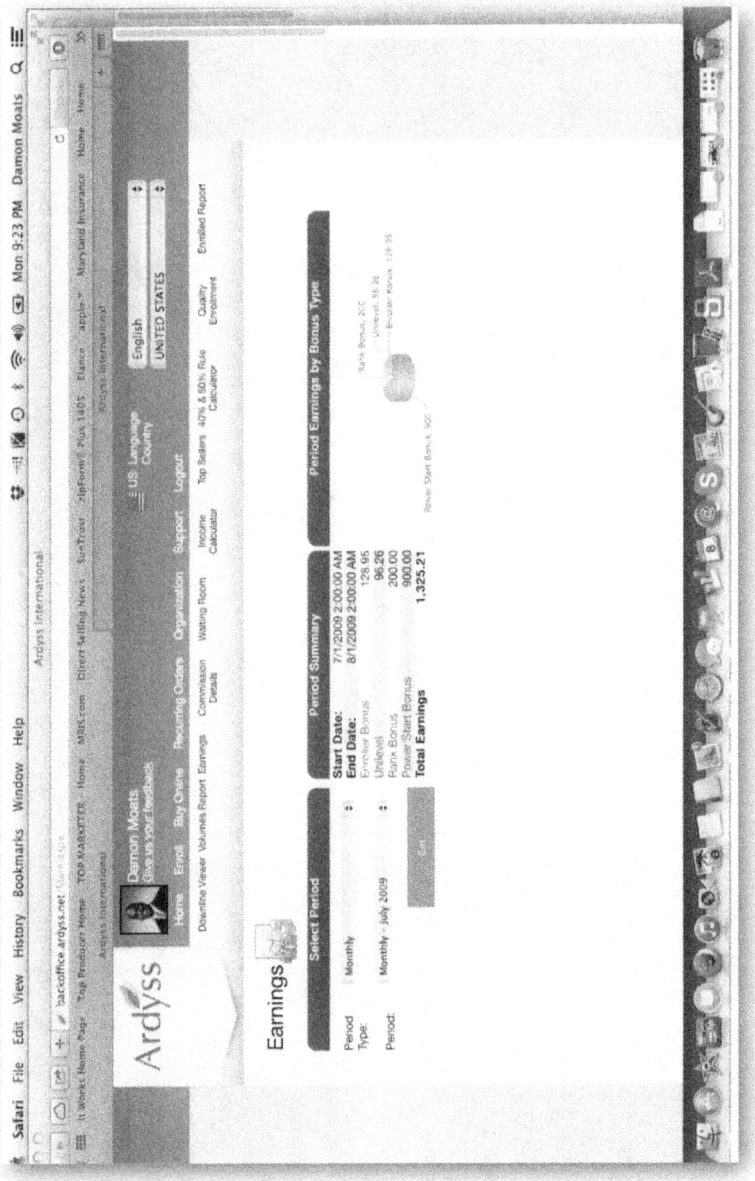

Exhibit 18

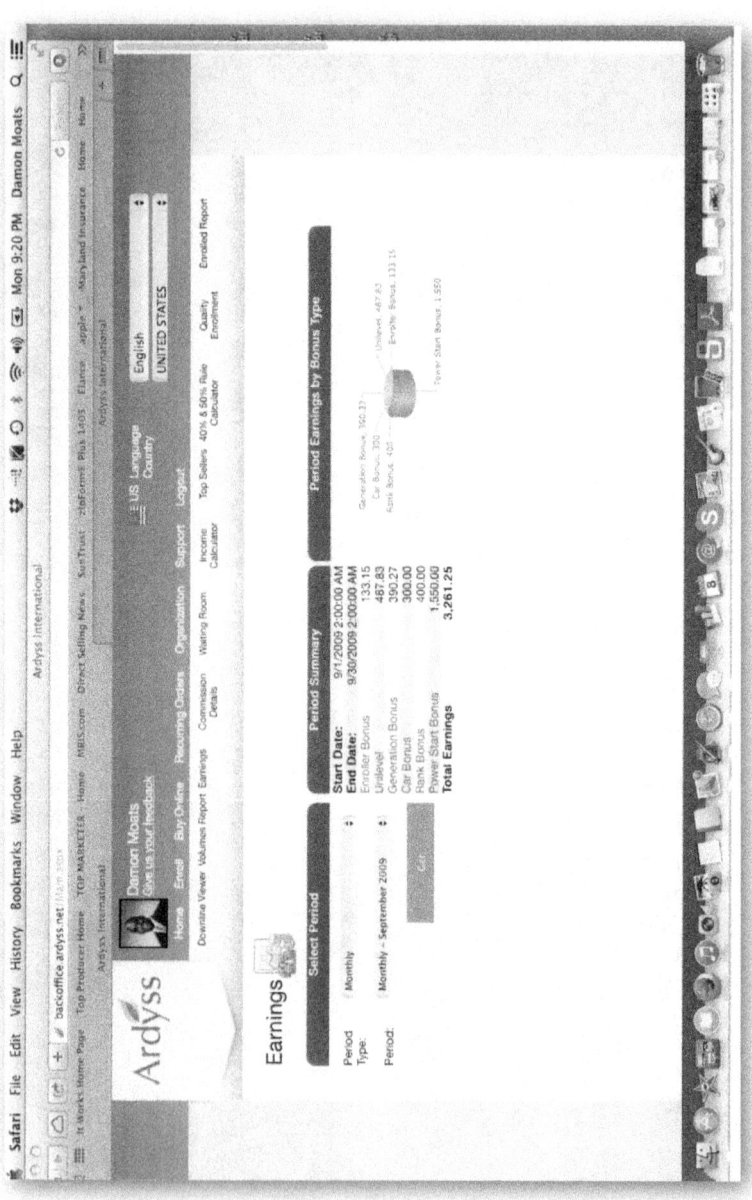

Exhibit 19

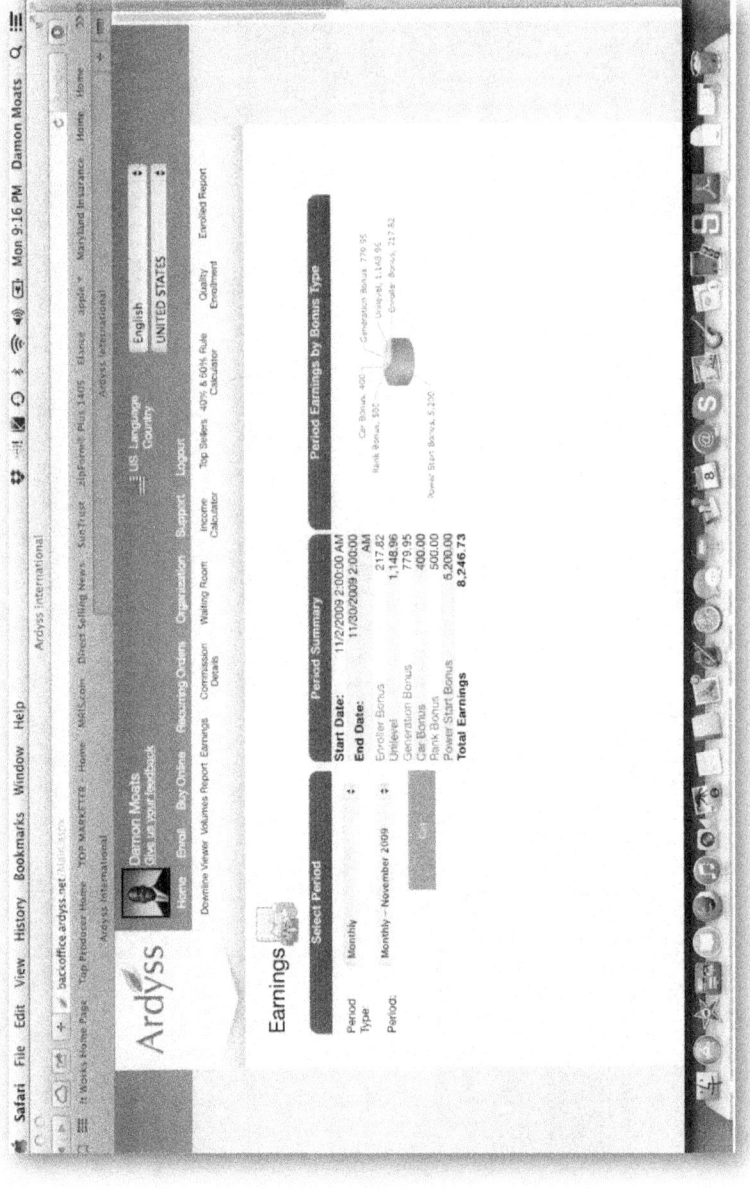

Exhibit 20

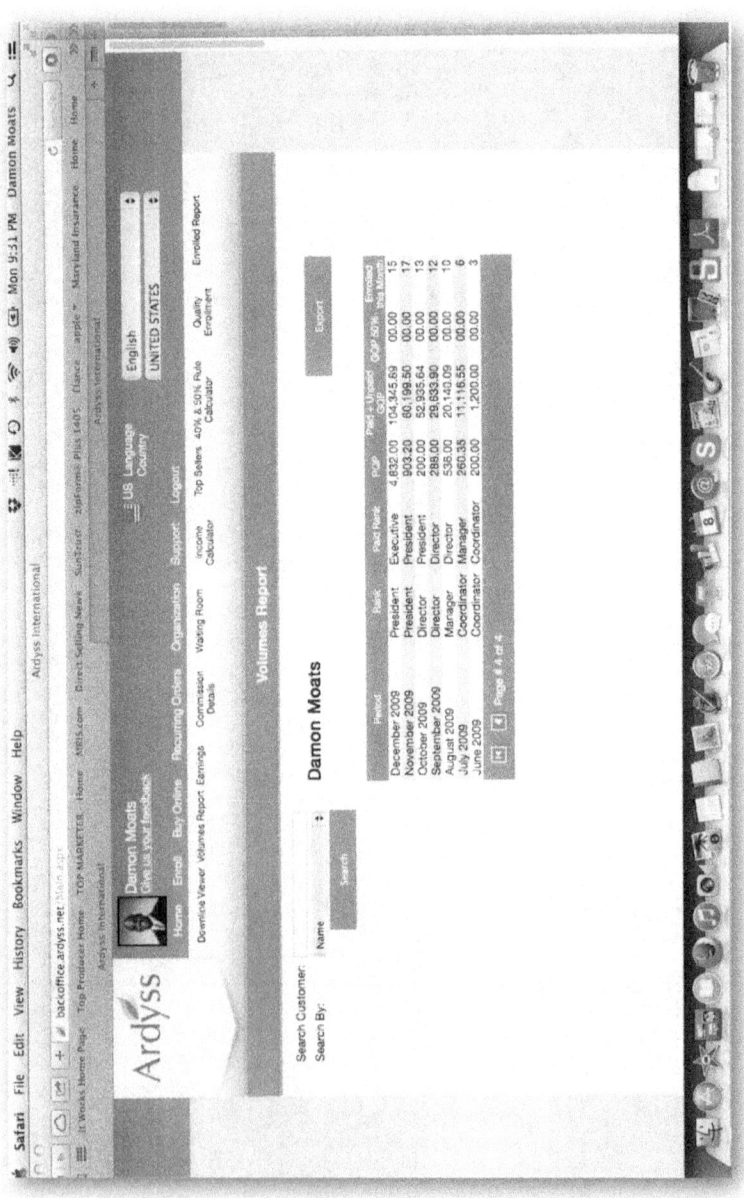

Exhibit 21

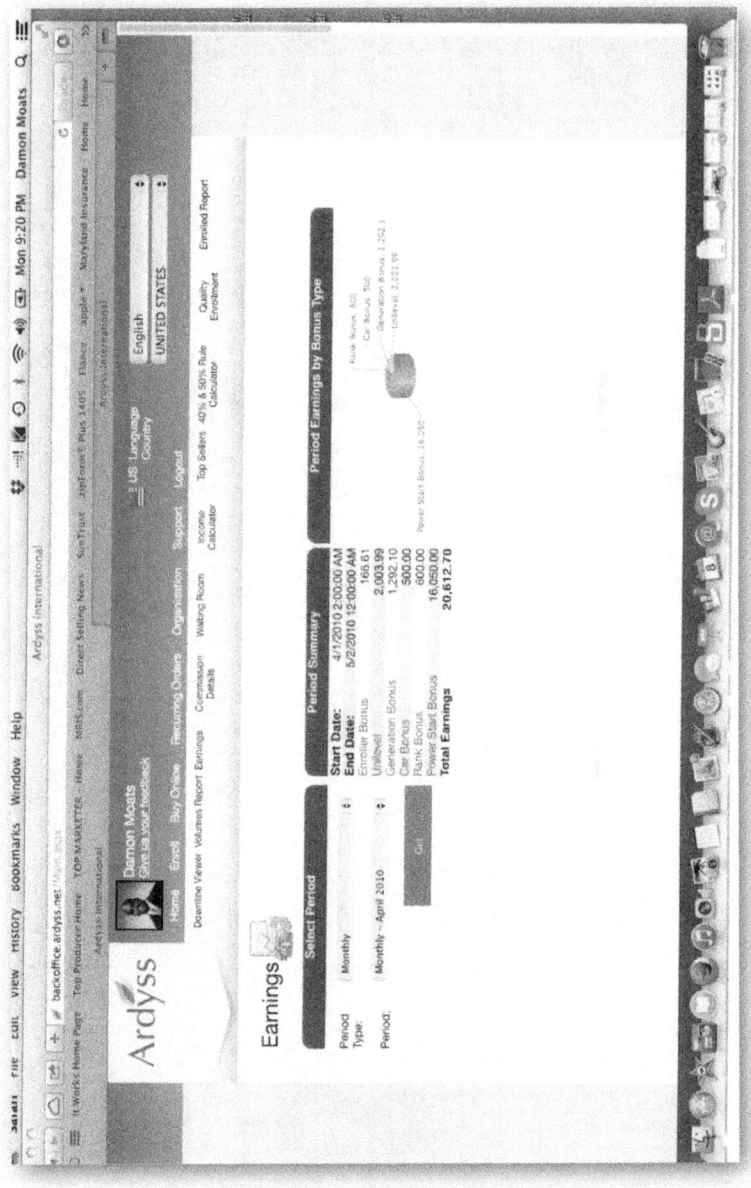

Exhibit 22

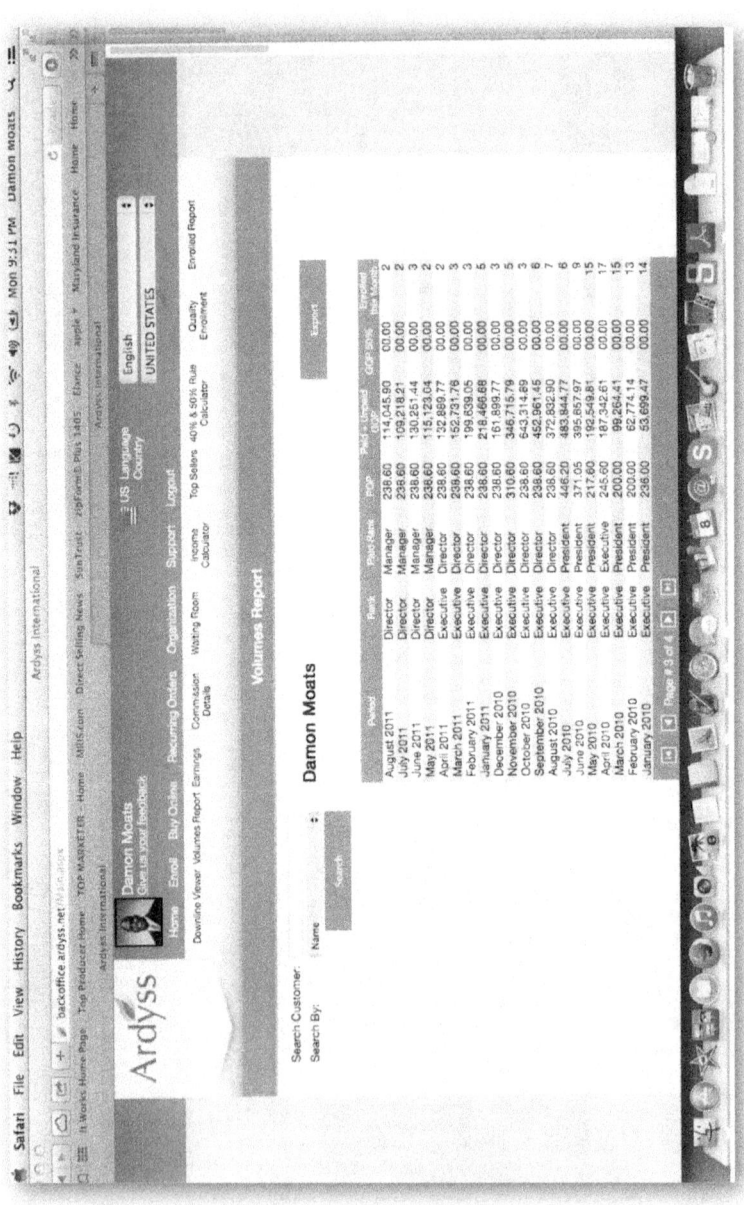

Exhibit 23

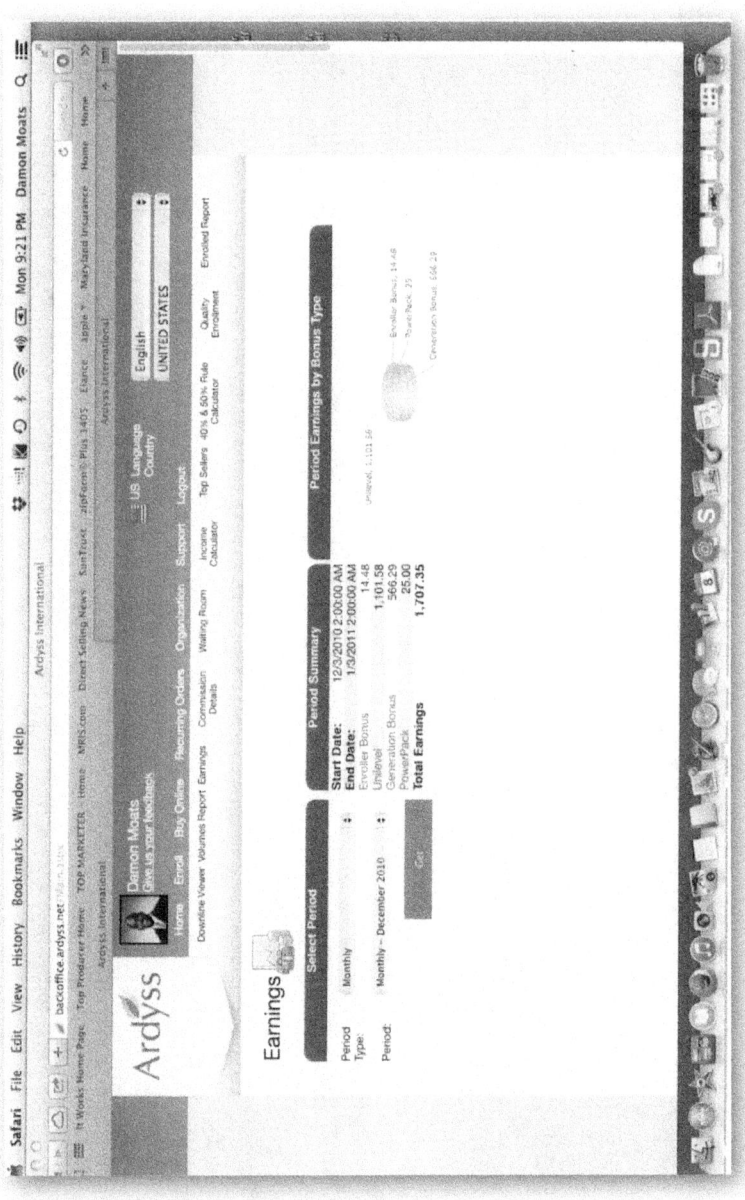

www.ingramcontent.com/pod-product-compliance
Lightning Source LLC
Chambersburg PA
CBHW051920170526
45168CB00001B/466